Red
World

and
White

Red World

MEMORIES OF A CHIPPEWA BOYHOOD
By JOHN ROGERS (CHIEF SNOW CLOUD)

and White

Foreword by Joseph W. Whitecotton

UNIVERSITY OF OKLAHOMA PRESS : NORMAN

Library of Congress Cataloging in Publication Data

Rogers, John, Chippewa chief.
    Red world and white.

    Published in 1957 under title: A Chippewa
speaks.
    1. Rogers, John, Chippewa chief. 2. Chippewa
Indians. I. Title.
E99.C6R633 1974   970.3 [B]   72–9263
ISBN 0–8061–1069–4   R63

To my loving wife, my father, my relatives, and friends —for their unfailing interest and the co-operation and encouragement I received in the preparation of this book.

By Joseph W. Whitecotton

FOREWORD

T HIS BOOK consists of recollections of a Chippewa Indian, focuses on his boyhood, and depicts the thinking and learning processes of a youth caught between two cultural worlds. Except for opening paragraphs, when the author is attending school in Flandreau, South Dakota, the events take place in the White Earth Reservation country of Minnesota. The Rice River, Mahnomen Beaulieu, White Earth (where he attended school the second time), Bagley (where he was born), and Cass Lake (where his father lived) are all located in this general region. The time span of the account covers the years from 1896, when Way Quauh Gishig was six years old, until the early years of the twentieth century, when he was nearing manhood.

The account may be interpreted on several levels. On one level it illustrates something about Chippewa culture of the time, presents ethnographic data about the Chippewas, most detailed on matters of subsistence economy, including techniques of hunting, house construction, and material culture. On another level it depicts a phenomenon known not only to the Chippewas, but found in a variety of situations—what happens to individuals when they face cultures different from their own and become the victims of rapid social and cultural change.

The Chippewas (or Ojibwas as they are sometimes called) belong to the Woodland culture area of North America; linguistically they are Algonquian speakers, a grouping which includes the Blackfeet, Cheyennes, and Arapahos as well as an Eastern and Central division. Chippewa belongs to the Central type of Algonquian languages, a classification it shares with the Cree-Montagnais, the Menomini, the Saulk, Shawnee, the Fox and Kickapoo, the Potawatomi, Ottawa, and others.

By the beginning of the nineteenth century, the Chippewas had reached their maximum expansion and occupied a vast territory including much of the region between the Lower Peninsula of Michigan, part of Ontario, and the eastern Saskatchewan plains. Four main divisions of Chippewa culture had emerged, and, because of contact with whites and other Indian groups in this area, a number of cultural adaptations were present.

The Plains Ojibwas (or Bungees) had adopted a bison-hunting economy and were very much like other Plains tribes in social and cultural features. The northern Chippewas (or Saulteaux) occupied the forest regions of the upland area north of the Great Lakes and resembled other forest Algonquians with their dependence on a hunting-gathering-fishing economy (excluding wild rice and maple sugar), a family hunting territorial system, and the prevalence of small family band organization. The southeastern Chippewas of peninsular Michigan and nearby Ontario formed more permanent summer villages and winter-extended family hunting bands and practiced farming, hunting, and fishing.

The southwestern Chippewas (with which this book deals) occupied the Lake Superior shore and interior Wisconsin and Minnesota, engaged in little farming and emphasized hunting and trapping along with the gathering of wild rice and maple sugar. As this account shows, some fishing was done in Minnesota, although it was secondary; the Chippewas on the Lake Superior shore placed more emphasis on this economic pursuit than did their more southerly neighbors.[1]

It is obvious from this account, as well as from the works of a number of anthropologists, that Chippewa culture and society had undergone a series of modifications since aboriginal times. This is true not only in some of the more obvious examples of material culture but also in the basic nature of the society itself. As late as the middle of the nineteenth century, among the Chippewas of Wisconsin and Minnesota, there was a number of "collective" or "corporate" organizations, including the village as a major political unit, joint hunting bands, and warrior societies accompanied by a council of chiefs.

With the institution of the reservation system by the United States government in the 1870's, Chippewa society underwent a fragmentation of "cor-

[1] Historical and ethnographic accounts of Chippewa culture and society are found in the works of Sister M. Inez Hilger, *Chippewa Child Life and Its Cultural Background* (Smithsonian Institution, Bureau of American Ethnology, *Bulletin 146* [1951]), and Harold Hickerson, *The Southwestern Chippewa: An Ethnohistorical Study* (American Anthropological Association, *Memoir 92* [1962]). Both works contain extensive bibliographies.

xi

porate" social groupings, a splintering that had already begun with the decline of the fur trade somewhat earlier and a cessation of hostilities between the Dakotas and the Chippewas—hostilities that had been brought on by the expansion of the fur trade in the 1730's. In short, Chippewa society and culture, by the time Rogers depicts it, was characterized by what anthropologists refer to as "structural atomism." In the words of Victor Barnouw, who studied the modern reservation Chippewas, "there was no economic cooperation outside the family unit. There was no communal hunting, no camp circle, no organized council of chiefs, no policing system, no regularly constituted military societies, and no symbols of group integration. Every man was for himself or for his own family; and there were few activities which linked the isolated families together."[2]

Many examples of this atomism may be gleaned from the words of John Rogers. In fact, his own family is typified by a brittleness characteristic of atomistic societies. His mother and father have parted company; it is only after his uncle's wife dies that his uncle becomes prominent in the story; adoption, or hoped-for adoption, of children in his own family is a common theme; the major institutional life for Chippewa children centers around the

[2] Victor Barnouw, *Acculturation and Personality Among the Wisconsin Chippewa* (American Anthropological Association, Memoir 72 [1950]), 16. Additional accounts of Chippewa atomism include Bernard J. James, "Social-Psychological Dimensions of Ojibwa Acculturation," *American Anthropologist* Vol. 63, No. 5, part 1 (1961).

school, controlled by outside authorities. Chippewa religious practices, which take place mostly within the contexts of sickness and death, are individualistic or atomized—there are no group ceremonials. Hunting and gathering are purely family enterprises. In the latter part of the book, when Way Quauh Gishig returns to his father, we do have an example of group ceremonialism. But, as we shall see below, this is revitalistic; the author does not realize that this movement is a "last ditch" effort to revive Chippewa society and culture.

Atomism is a structural phenomenon found in a wide variety of cultural contexts and is by no means restricted to Chippewa society or to the contact between American Indians and Euroamerican culture. It has been noted among peasants in Mexico and southern Italy, in Melanesia and among urban blacks, Mexican-Americans, and Italian-Americans. It seems to occur most frequently when state political institutions permeate all areas of a society, incorporating in their wake diverse cultural forms. In such contexts, village or local-level institutions are incapable of competing with far-flung bureaucracies and become extinct.

Because the cultural worlds in which they operate are different from those of the competing state-level institutions, the peoples so affected must surrender control to a state political form in which they do not participate, which they do not understand, and with which they lack the means to cope. In short, they lack access to the resources of the society in which they find themselves suddenly embedded. This is frequently countered with a strong egalitarian ethic, with a reluctance to co-operate with other individuals in their own communities, leading to an absence of concerted action and inter-personal relationships characterized by restraint, reserve, and suspicion. Their society becomes fragmented and marginal, as do the psychological profiles of the men who compose it.[3]

John Rogers as an individual illustrates this wider process. Thus this document is not only a Chippewa document, but more importantly a human one—a document that depicts a man caught between two worlds—one Indian, one white, or, as he expresses it, the world of nature and the world of the book.

There are certain common characteristics of these marginal men; they may completely reject the old world, the world of their ancestors, or they may experience a blind, passionate nostalgia for it. The former occurs most frequently in situations of immigration, as when European peasants migrated to this country around the turn of the century; the latter more frequently occurs under conditions described in this account.

But one must be wary of such generalizations, for the two may develop in a single individual at different points in his lifetime. Since Chief Snow Cloud wrote this account late in life looking back on his childhood, we do not know to what extent the first

[3] The best accounts of the atomistic type of society can be found in various papers in a special issue of the journal *Human Organization*, Vol. 27, No. 3 (1968), entitled "Perspectives on the Atomistic Type Society."

process may have occurred in him; but from the account we have ample evidence for the second.

John Rogers' reaction to another culture reminds one of other such men. Pedro Martínez, depicted by Oscar Lewis in his masterful book of that name, is a Mexican peasant caught between the world of the *pueblo*, disintegrating before his very eyes, and the world of the Mexican nation.[4] Juan the Chamula, presented to us by Ricardo Pozas, finds himself in a similar situation as a Tzotzil Indian enmeshed in a world he poorly understands.[5] All of these accounts have even more impact on the reader because they are presented in the words of the individuals themselves; they create for us a time capsule, one we can enter to hear the spoken words of marginal, sometimes desperate, individuals crying out for understanding and appreciation.

While he seems to develop some sympathies for the new world, John adopts a nostalgia for the world of his ancestors; he sees the contrast between the old ways and the new in most vivid terms—a contrast that permeates every level of his observations. The impact is even more striking, not only because he is speaking as if he were a child, but also because he imperfectly understands either world and is trying to learn about both.

Near the end of the account, John finds, and becomes infatuated with, the ceremonialism of Chip-

[4] Oscar Lewis, *Pedro Martínez: A Mexican Peasant and His Family* (New York, Random House, 1964) .

[5] Ricardo Pozas, *Juan the Chamula* (Berkeley, University of California Press, 1966) .

pewa culture and a document, describing the old ways, which his father shows him. While this imbues him with a desire to preserve his Indian culture, it is clear that many things in it are not aboriginal Chippewa. The document and ceremonialism he describes are associated with the Midewiwin movement, a Chippewa nativistic movement which contains elements of both Christian and native Indian belief.[6] Such movements frequently occur under conditions of stress; they attempt to recreate what is lost even though they combine, almost willy-nilly, aspects of different cultures—a combination that is not necessarily understood as such by the participants.[7]

This also is a common phenomenon among men under cultural stress; they share a common destiny and develop a common fate. Perhaps such men realize that they can never return, in a real sense, to the world that has been lost. They realize, if only reluctantly, that their culture is "going to hell in a handbasket." They know it is doomed, but they nevertheless long for it. In the process, the old becomes perfect, almost utopian. It is as if the utopia of man has passed, and they must make it come again, if only in their minds, and with whatever cultural baggage they can conjure up.

[6] The Midewiwin is dealt with in Harold Hickerson, *The Chippewa and Their Neighbors* (New York, Holt, Rinehart and Winston, 1970), 51–63.

[7] Anthony F. C. Wallace, "Revitalization Movements: Some Theoretical Considerations for Their Comparative Study," *American Anthropologist*, Vol. 58 (1956), 264–81, is the basic paper on this subject.

But we should not scoff at such re-creations, for they are not merely passing fancies or examples of exotica. We are all creatures of a rapidly changing world, where societies and the individuals who compose them are placed under constant stress. Modern-day examples, such as the black movement, the Chicano movement, the movement for women's liberation, and various youth movements, all conjure up images of utopian social justice. Their occurrence at a time when American culture has taken on a pluralistic fragmentation should remind us that rapid culture change should not be relegated to the backroads of history. As social scientists, we need to understand more fully the dynamics of groups and individuals enmeshed in the process of rapid social and cultural change; as human beings we need to recognize the universal plight of man as he faces an unknown world not of his own making. This account by John Rogers should assist us in both of these endeavors.

Red
World

and
White

A Chippewa Speaks

CHAPTER I

I, WAY QUAH GISHIG, was six years old when my two sisters, Bishiu and Min di, accompanied me to Flanreau, South Dakota to attend an Indian boarding school.

It was very difficult for me at first, for students at the school were not allowed to speak the language of the Indians. At that time I understood nothing else.

Neither did I like to be forced to remain with my sisters in the girls' building instead of being assigned to the quarters occupied by the boys.

I was as shy and timid as the young buck in the forest and clung very closely to my sister. But soon I learned to speak and understand a little of the white man's language; and gradually the boys began coaxing me to play with them.

At first I wore my hair in two braids, Indian fashion, but at last my sisters gave in and allowed it to be cut so that I would be like the other boys.

My many happy years at the school have no place in this volume, so I will begin at the time Min di, Bishiu, and I took the train to return home.

Min di, who at school was given the name of Caroline, was tall and slender as the sapling pine. Her eyes as soft and innocent as a doe's. She wore her raven black hair loose, hanging down her back, and tied with a buckskin string.

We got off the puffing, snorting train at Mah-nomen. There a man named John Carr met us. He put us in his light wagon. Min di sat on the seat beside him, and Bishiu and I alternately stood or lay down in the rear.

With ever widening interest we stared off at the passing landscape. The road wound along ahead of us, turning and curling like a slithering serpent.

I was anxious to see my mother and be home again, but even this strong desire could not keep me awake for so many hours, and finally Weeng, the sleep spirit, settled down over me.

We stopped briefly at the town of Beaulieu, where we got out and stretched our legs and had lunch. When we started out again, the scene was changed. We came into wooded places, where trees seem to tower upward to the sky and cast deep dark shadows on the fallen leaves encircling them.

Finally Min di turned and exclaimed, "Look, Way quah!" She pointed toward the north.

There in the distance I saw the sparkle of water and the ripple of waves as the sun was reflected back through the trees. This I knew was home!

Coming to a halt near a wigwam, the driver got down and helped us out.

"Here we are, children. Over there is your mother."

He did not mention my father, and I wondered about him.

Mother was seated on the ground, working on some fish nets. She was heavy and broad, but her hands and feet were small. Her hair, straight and

4

black, was tied with a red string. She wore a full-skirted blue calico dress, with long blousey sleeves, a low neck, and a tight-fitting waist. Her waist was encircled by a fringed belt with red, yellow green, and blue figures in it.

I learned later that mother had to keep very busy making linen-thread fish nets to sell—for now she had extra mouths to feed.

She looked up from her work, and we children made a mad scramble toward her. As she stood up with outstretched arms her eyes sparkled as does the sun on laughing waters.

What a reunion that was! She endeavored to gather us all into her arms at once. She started talking joyously, but we couldn't understand very well what she said, for we had forgotten much of the Indian language during our six years away from home.

But all that mattered was we were welcome here in mother's wigwam—the home of our birth.

After supper that evening Mother took us back to where the nets were, and there was our new baby brother, Ahmeek (meaning "beaver") .

I had known nothing about him until then. But there he was, lying in his cradle, which looked something like a white man's hammock strung between two trees. It was situated conveniently so that mother could reach out as she sat making nets and swing him back and forth, and croon to him to the accompaniment of the wind that rustled in the towering pines.

I stood staring down at my baby brother, and suddenly he looked up at me with his pretty dark eyes, raised his chubby little hands, and gurgled happily. To me he was saying, "Aren't you proud of your new little brother?"

His hair was straight and dark. He wore a little red and white checked calico dress.

Bishiu, now fourteen years of age, came up to me. She was tall for her age, but shorter and heavier than Min di. She had teasing brown eyes and was very pretty. She still wore the uniform of the school —a white blouse and blue skirt, with high-buttoned shoes and black stockings. She always liked the dress of the white people.

Bishiu bent over the cradle and held out her arms to her new baby brother.

"Min di said I should bring him to the wigwam," she said, "and you are to help Mother straighten out her nets."

Mother, who sat nearby, shook her head.

"No, we will go into the wigwam now."

She picked up her pipe and kinnikinic (Indian tobacco), and we all went into the wigwam. It was about the size of a large room in a white man's dwelling. In the center was a fireplace, and above in the middle of the roof was an opening for light and for the smoke to escape. Suspended from a framework over the fire were two kettles almost full of water.

On one side of this large room I saw a bedframe made of poles. Over these were laid boughs to make a smooth, springly couch about the size of a double bed. The bedding consisted of deer pelts and, when not in use, could be folded back to the wall and serve as a back-rest.

Along the east wall was mother's workshop, and opposite the door the kitchen equipment was kept. On the west side was a place for the man's work-shop. Over at the opposite wall was the pit used for storing and the wood pile. The storage pit was a hole dug in the ground, and this was overlaid with hay, on top of which was some birch bark. Here were potatoes, carrots, corn, onions, and any canned or dried fruits that had accumulated from the gather of fruits and berries.

I wondered where I was to sleep during that first night at home, for I could see but one bed. After awhile I questioned Min di, and she answered in Indian fashion:

"For the time, while our earth mother is still warm, you will sleep outside under the trees. But later, when the thunder clouds bring the rains, you will have another bed on the opposite side of the room."

I was then instructed what to do to prepare the outside bed. They told me to get four poles and place them upright in the ground. From the four corners thus formed a netting was draped down over the sides to protect me from mosquitos and other insects during the time when darkness reigned and man dwelt under the spell of the sleep spirit.

During the days that followed we had a happy time getting acquainted after those long years of separation. Mother kept saying what a big help I was going to be. She asked whether I thought I would be happy gathering birch bark, tobacco, and wood? I was pleased to feel that I would grow into a strong young brave, and so I tried very hard to please her and to learn once more the Chippewa language. Min di was the only one who could speak both the Chippewa and English tongues, so for a time she interpreted all that mother said to Bishiu and me.

Mother promised to teach me the ways of the forest, rivers, and lakes—how to set rabbit snares and deadfalls, how to trap for wolves and other wild animals that roamed this land of the Chippewas.

While we sat around the fire talking and planning, Mother told my oldest sister to explain that she wanted us to be called by our Indian names. She insisted that we start at once to use them. So Min di told us not ever to use our school names any more. And so we became Min di and Bishiu, my two sisters, and Ahmeek, which meant "beaver" (the baby). My own Indian name, Way Quah, meant "dawn of day" and at school I was known as John.

CHAPTER II

AT THE TIME of my homecoming I was twelve years old and quite tall for my age. I was straight as a pine. My hair was black and wavy, and my eyes sharp and brown.

I generally kept very quiet when in the presence of people.

Mother was very clever and direct in teaching me the Indian way of things. One day she called out abruptly: "Way quah, get those rocks and floats out by the tree. They are tied with wegoob."

Wegoob is the green inner bark from the basswood tree. This I got immediately, as mother watched me. I picked the rocks she wanted, which were about the size of a wild-duck egg, and the floats, which were made of cedar. I carried them into the wigwam and Mother and Min di arranged them on the nets.

"And now," said Mother approvingly, "get a hatchet and come with me down the beach to our nearest neighbor. There we will borrow a canoe to use for setting the nets."

As we walked along, she pointed to some red willow. She cut some of this to show me how, and took it along with us.

I shall never forget the experience in the borrowed canoe. This was my first ride in a boat made of birch bark. Mother put me in front, and we paddled back to our landing.

Mother frequently smoked a pipe, and I wondered where she got it and whether I could make one like it. So I asked her, and she explained that when a young girl she had gone with Chief Bay mi chig gah nany (meaning "Long Lake"), and he it was who had given the pipe to her. It had been handed down from chief to chief, until it finally came to him and he then told her that it was now hers.

"And so, Way quah," she said, "when you have

grown to be a strong young brave, this pipe shall be yours." And to this day I have it among my prized possessions.

The peace pipe is made of black stone, and has a round bowl on a square base. It is inlaid with red stone and lead. The stem is made from the ash tree that grows in the swamps.

Often when Mother and all of us would sit around the fire, she would tell us stories of the Chippewas and about our brother and sister who were away at school in Morris, Minnesota; a brother and sister I would see again after the robin returned and the sun began once more to melt the snows and warm the earth.

This was the first time I knew I had two brothers and three sisters. I envisioned the fun we would all have playing on the shore of the lake and swimming in its smiling, rippling waters.

In Mother's stories were many interesting facts about our Grandmother. Mother promised we would go to her for a visit before many more suns. She hadn't seen us since we left for school.

It was early morning of a day in the following week that we started on this visit.

We took with us some mosquito netting and enough food to last for a few days. This was quite a load for us to pack, for we also had little Ahmeek to carry, and Grandmother's house was some six miles distant on a different trail.

We traveled slowly, but enjoyed every step of the way. The call of the birds and the voices of other wild things were like music to my ears. It seemed that the trees and shrubs were whispering messages and that the Great Spirit hovered very near on this trail where the shadows were deep. Now and then we would see a deer or a rabbit, or perhaps, it would be a squirrel that would scamper up the tree and scold us for intruding upon his peaceful domain.

Coming at last to the house, we dropped our packs outside. Mother's sister came to the door and greeted us with open arms. Grandma's face lighted up when she saw who it was. She seemed to be a very happy person, and she had been blessed with a very long life. She opened her heart to us instantly and made us feel at home while we remained in her dwelling.

When at last we were ready for the return trip through the forest trail, mother's sister offered to drive us home. Mother and Min di were never idle. They fashioned many useful articles with strips of birch bark peeled from nearby trees. From the sweet grass various roots and bulrushes were obtained. Then there were mats, baskets, and little birch-bark canoes.

In the gathering of rushes, Mother made us go out into the deep water where we would dive for the longer rushes. The longer the better, she told us; for the longer ones made larger and finer mats. Articles she made this way could be traded for flour, sugar, and other food supplies.

Now the time of the melting snows had come and gone. Soft, gentle winds warmed the earth. Summer was well along. We gathered birch bark for Mother, and with this she would make containers and dishes for our winter supplies. To remove this bark from the trees required skill in order not to harm the bark. If we cut too deeply it would leave a scar, for the new bark would not again grow out smooth.

Mother was careful to teach us just how it was done. With a sharp knife we would cut through the inner bark only. Indeed, it seemed that the Great Spirit had placed it there to let us know just how deeply to cut. It was our code never to destroy anything that Nature had given us. If we took care in stripping the bark, more would be provided on the same tree.

At the coming of the robin was the best season for getting the bark, but since Mother had time now, in the fall, to teach us, she felt there was no need to wait.

While the leaf was still brown on the forest trees and the cold north wind had yet to bring the snow to our village, a young brave named Wa goosh came to our wigwam and asked Mother to come to the church of the white man, for a prayer meeting.

Mother looked upon Wa goosh with favor. He seemed to be always about when needed and always willing to help.

When Wa goosh first saw my sister Min di, it was plain that he liked her and it was the beginning of a beautiful friendship.

Wa goosh (meaning "fox") was tall and strong. He was the typical Chippewa brave. His shirt was tan and of buckskin, open at the throat and with long sleeves and beautifully beaded cuffs. His trousers were dark and soft as the forest moss. Knotted about his throat he wore a colored silk handkerchief. But he wore no hat and no earrings. Usually there was just a band about his forehead and his hair hung in two braids.

I learned that Wa goosh was a hunter, a farmer, and a blacksmith, and would gather herbs beneficial to the sick. For these he would never accept pay, saying that those who were helped in their sickness could pay him with gifts if they chose to do so.

One morning Wa goosh asked Mother:

"Have the children ever seen a squaw dance?"

"No, Wa goosh, they haven't," she answered.

"Then at the time of the next dance you are all to go with me."

"We will come," Mother promised.

Thus it was when the Indians next gathered for this great occasion of the dance, we went with Wa goosh. We had heard that he was counted as one of the best solo dancers on the White Earth reservation. In his beautiful costume the young brave made the heart of every Indian maiden beat with desire to win his favor. But apparently he was most pleased when Min di joined him in the dance.

It is the custom at the squaw dance for the male to offer a gift to the girl with whom he wishes to perform, such as a handkerchief or goods for a new dress or maybe an article of food she would like. If she accepts, then she dances with him; and if she desires another dance with him, she gives him something in return. This might be a pair of beaded gloves or beaded cuffs. Or perhaps any beaded article that she owns and believes may please the young brave of her choice.

Here at the dance it was also the custom to exchange articles. If one wanted a pony that would pair with one he owned, he would offer his costume in exchange. The arrangement is made through one of his people, and they too join in the dance.

After a time they sit at the edge of the circle. Next comes the solo dance—without partners. Single dancers weave in and out and around one another, always circling the drummers, who are in the center. Only the men take part in this, and it is very rhythmic and beautiful. Then, after a time, he who has received the costume arises to announce that he will give his pony for it.

I shall never forget that first squaw dance that I attended. Thereafter, I never missed another one.

And so the long white winter passed. The snows melted from field and forest. Birds appeared in the budding trees and their song gladdened the hearts of all who heard.

CHAPTER III

WHILE PLAYING with Ahmeek one morning, Bishiu and I were swinging him in his cradle when we heard a wagon deep in the forest. A little later it came into view, bringing a man, a woman, and two children. We ran into the wigwam to our sister, Min di, and asked her who it could be. She and mother came out.

"Why, it's your brother and sister—Mah ni do mi naince and Osh kin nah way!" exclaimed Mother.

They were back from school. We boys stood there and admired each other's coats. Boylike, we compared them and found them very much alike, both having brass buttons and buttoned right up to the neck. The rest of Osh kin nah way's costume was a lot like mine too—blue-gray short trousers, high shoes, and black stockings.

He was ten years old, short and chubby, with black hair and brown eyes. He was very bashful. We called him Osh kin for short.

Mah ni do mi naince was twelve, tall and slender, but not very strong. She had long dark hair, braided to fall in front and tied with a red ribbon. Her eyes were brown. Her uniform was a jumper skirt of blue and a white blouse, high shoes, and black stockings. We called her Mah ni.

Neither could talk Indian. So I felt sorry for them. They would have to learn the Indian tongue all over again, the same as Bishiu and I had to do. I felt I could be of much help to them.

The four of us children would make birchbark baskets and take them out to fill with berries. There were strawberries, raspberries, high bush cranberries, wild grapes, and blueberries, for it was the time of their ripening.

If we had more than we could eat, Mother would

dry them out in the sun, then put them away for use when the cold, icy days of the winter came.

Soon came the time for the leaves to turn brown and yellow and gold. The forest was beautiful and the wind rustled the dry leaves. We just couldn't resist the temptation to gather those beautiful colored leaves and the empty birds' nests.

At school, if we brought in a nest or a pretty leaf, we were given much credit, and we thought we would also please Mother by bringing some to her. But she did not like our doing this. She would scold and correct us and tell us we were destroying something—that the nests were the homes of the birds and the leaves were the beauty of the forest.

I loved to lie on my back under the trees and watch the clouds forming and moving. Sometimes it seemed they were so swift in their movements I would wonder where they were going. And then at other times they would just hang there, like great white doves.

With the coming of night, Mother would teach us how to make dishes out of birch bark. When we went on camping trips, having no horses, we were able to take only the necessary pots and supplies, so it was urgent that we understood how to make our own dishes.

These we fashioned as we needed them, for always did we carry birch bark with us. Sometimes we had soup, and this would call for deeper dishes. The dishes were always burned after each meal—no washing and nothing left around to attract bugs or flies.

We had so much to learn. Mother taught us how to get larger strips of birch bark, up to eighteen or thirty-six inches. This had to be taken from a tree about six inches through, making a strip some eighteen inches wide and as long as we wanted to strip them. They were sewed together to make a strip about twelve to eighteen feet long and thirty-six inches wide. The raw edges were in thirty-six-inch-widths and bound with cedar and sewed with basswood bark. This prevented breaking and tearing when rolled. Ten or twelve sheets like this were sufficient to cover a wigwam.

The rolls were very light in weight. The wigwam frame was made by pushing long poles into the ground about sixteen inches apart and bending and tying them together at the top with basswood bark. These were covered with birch-bark strips, starting at the bottom by the door opening and working around the bottom and upwards.

There is always an opening about three by five feet right in the center of the top, as we were taught that light which came directly down from the abode of the Great Spirit was better for us. It served as an outlet for the smoke from our fires also.

In order to keep the fires burning with the least trouble, Mother taught us the kind of wood to gather that would not throw off sparks and set our clothing or bedding on fire while we slept. The logs were cut larger and greener for the base of the fire, to keep the ashes and hot coals together. The night fire was always made with hardwoods limbs, oak or ash, as these burned slower and had no flame and not much smoke. We never expected the fire to last all night, but it would keep the base of the fireplace warm so it wouldn't take long to heat up and allowed a good hearth of coals for baking a fish or fowl for the noonday meal.

The way we prepared fish for baking in the ashes of an open fire was to clean and dress them, cutting out the gills and slitting down the back from the head, leaving the head and scales on and taking out the insides. The fish were then carefully packed in clay, about the thickness of a child's hand, and buried quite deep near the base of the coals. The fire must not be too hot.

It required about half a morning or more to bake them. But when they were taken from the fire and clay, the scales would cling to the clay, so the fish were all ready to eat. And, oh, how delicious they were!

The manner of cooking partridges and ducks was a little different. After cleaning and dressing them, they were packed in clay and buried in the ashes head down, with rocks between them and the fire, so the feet would not burn off. When the feet, if jerked gently, would pull away, the fowl was done.

Mother had accepted the kind offer of Wa goosh to take us to the rice beds. So she made for Osh kin and me "rice moccasins." These were made to fit higher and snugger around the foot and ankle, to prevent the rice husks from getting in.

Finally we were ready to go. It was quite a job

getting everything from the wigwam down to the lake shore, a job for us children.

It was decided that Mother and Wa goosh would first take all of the supplies in the canoe, heading towards the river, up the river, across the lake, up another river, and then into the rice beds.

They found the place where Mother wanted to camp and then came back for us. This took from sun to sun.

The first night we slept under the stars, for we had no time to make a wigwam before darkness fell. We thought this was a lot of fun.

With the first morning light Wa goosh took us two boys out to cut down about thirty long poles for the wigwam. We dragged them to the location of the camp. Min di, Mother, and Wa goosh set them up. Then Mother and Min di took the birch bark, which was light, and covered the poles. They tied the bark firmly around the poles so the wind could not easily blow it off.

Our next chore was to get wood for the fires. We gathered enough to last three or four days.

It was the dark of the moon, so Wa goosh suggested that Mother and he go on a fire hunt. This meant he would have to return to his home and get the canoe to be used for the hunt. It was smaller and would be much better for the rice beds too, for the smaller the canoe the less parting in the rice grains. Four could sit in it easily, but even six could ride.

Like all children we begged to go along, and

finally Wa goosh consented. We had made little paddles of our own and were dying to use them. Running to get these, we came back and sat in the middle of the canoe and in our rather futile way helped to paddle.

Back over the lake we glided, then down the river into another lake, the waters of which were like glass. But it was beautiful, and we could see the reflection of the shoreline all around. It seemed that we actually skimmed over the water, it was so smooth.

At last we arrived at the lake near Wa goosh's home. He pulled the big canoe up on shore and covered it with twigs and boughs. He told us he wanted us to come up to meet his Mother and Father. This we did as well as snooping around his place. We discovered many interesting things and were astonished at the different kinds of tools he had. I decided with a workshop like this I could build a canoe as graceful as a swan—and some time I would!

We came down again to the shore where Wa goosh uncovered the smaller canoe and pushed it into the water. The difference in size was as that of a mother swan and her young.

By this time the wind had risen and the lake was getting rough, as though the water manito were displeased. Min di and Wa goosh went to the shore.

"Maybe it won't be too bad," they said, "for the wind is blowing in the right direction to be in our backs."

As they came down to get in the canoe, Wa goosh

had a box on a pole. It looked like a reflector. This he put in the canoe with us. Sister told us this was what he was going to use in his fire hunt.

Wa goosh and Min di were well trained at the paddles and so the water's roughness did not bother us. We crossed the lake in good time, then into the river again. While paddling along, Wa goosh told Sister that he would teach us how to make bows and arrows—and might one day take us out for a hunt.

When we got back to the wigwam, Mother's face was like a storm cloud. She didn't like to have us always wanting to do everything Wa goosh planned. He was a man and we were still little fellows.

After our evening meal around the fire, Mother told Min di she wanted to relate a story about our father. This was in the Indian language, and Min di had to translate it to us in English. We were much excited. Mother started off:

"Your Father was a very brave hunter and a good provider. He knew the woods and lakes, and the habits of different animals. We made our canoe ready by placing a box like a reflector on a pole four feet long. This was placed in the bow of the canoe, so he could sight the game. A lantern was set in the boxlike structure throwing the light forward.

"He rowed over to the location where we might sight some deer, and then I took over the paddle. My task was to keep the canoe headed toward shore, so the light would attract the deer. Then he would be prepared to shoot when he saw the two fiery eyes.

"I guess I'm very good at this, for the least ripple

from a paddle or the scraping of the paddle on the canoe would scare the animals and cause them to dart into the safety of the forest.

"Suddenly we heard a strange noise. It didn't sound like a deer or a large animal. I stopped paddling. Never had we heard anything like it, and Father turned his head quickly. Neither one of us spoke—just listened, wondering what it was.

"Finally Father motioned for me to pull closer to the shore. I obeyed, and as we advanced I saw that the object was a porcupine—probably just coming down to drink. Father and I looked at one another. We both knew that meeting a porcupine at night was not a good omen. Should we catch him or let him go? Finally Father whispered: 'Let's get him and put him in the canoe. I want to get some venison. We'll take a chance on our good luck.'

"Your Father got out on the shore, seized a club and prepared to kill the porcupine. This accomplished, he loaded it into the canoe, and we continued paddling around looking for a deer.

"Before long we heard a splashing sound. Your Father looked at me. I shook my head and nodded. He pointed out the direction toward which I should paddle the canoe. As we approached I had to be very careful the light didn't move from side to side nor flicker. We both sat very still. He had put his paddle in the bottom of the canoe and was ready with his gun. Then we saw that it was a great moose."

As Mother talked, we children forgot all about what we were so eager to hear, about the trouble that had made Mother and Father forget the love that had once brought them together. We listened eagerly to know what would happen next in the story.

"I wondered why your father didn't shoot," continued Mother. "Then he whispered that he must get close enough to kill it with one shot, for the gun was loaded with buckshot.

"Finally we got close enough, and he took a shot at the moose and almost at the same instant put out the light. He thought at first he had killed the moose with one shot, but now we heard it coming our way. We realized we were in for a fight.

"I turned the canoe around quickly and headed it out to deeper water. But the beast, being wounded, made a lunge and came right out after us. He lashed the canoe to pieces, and we were both thrown into the lake. Luckily the beast didn't mangle us. We swam to shore while the moose turned to go back. But he bled to death before he could make it.

"We returned home, but the next day we borrowed a canoe and went back to where the moose had died. The lake was like glass and at the bottom of it we could see the gun, the sack of cartridges, and the lantern. We pulled the moose from the water and dressed him, then loaded him into the canoe. Father retrieved the gun and dried it out and as he looked at the shells, he saw that instead of buckshot the gun was loaded with fine shot, suitable for smaller game.

" 'No wonder we met the porcupine,' he said

to me. 'We were not prepared with the right shot. Surely the Great Spirit was watching over us.' "

Mother stopped in her story to be sure that we understood if anything out of the ordinary ever happened, like meeting a porcupine, we must be sure to take warning.

Mother went on to tell of how they got the meat home, but before she had finished, sleep had made our eyes heavy.

The next morning we awoke to see a deer strung up in a tree. It was then that Wa goosh told us how, in the dead of night, he and Mother had gone out on the fire hunt. He had used his box, and when they got to the location, Mother kept the canoe pointed to the shore, sliding along until the light attracted the deer. It was then Wa goosh had a chance to shoot. By good luck he had killed a big buck. Mother and he loaded it into the canoe and rowed it home. It was two o'clock in the morning by then, and before going to sleep they had been forced to skin and dress it.

Later that day we built a fire out of doors. Over this we fashioned a rack to hang the rice kettles on. Higher over this was another rack on which the deer meat could be dried.

While Wa goosh was cutting the venison, Osh kin and I were very alert, watching him. We noticed how he cut it up into long strips, as thick as a good steak and as long as he could cut them. The smoke kept the flies away. These strips were hung over the poles to dry in the sun and to absorb the heat from the fire and sun. The meat shrank a lot. This worried me, because I thought it would become tough. But Mother explained:

"It will be good for your teeth, having to chew the food well. It will make your teeth stronger and you can use them longer."

CHAPTER IV

MOTHER and Wa goosh started before daybreak for the rice beds. When they returned they had a nice load of rice. It was our job to bring it to the place where our large kettles were on the fire. We used birch-bark baskets and laid the rice out on a large sheet of birch bark. All the rice thus gathered was piled there for the day, about eight bushels of it.

Gathering rice is very interesting work. One person stands in front of the canoe. With a long, forked pole he slowly pushes the boat forward. The other person sits in the rear of the craft and, with two sticks made for this purpose, takes the grass and with one motion pulls it over the canoe. He then thrashes the grain, which falls into the boat.

When the boat is full, the one in front poles the load into deep water where he puts the pole away and paddles across the lake to shore. There the rice is hauled up to camp to the kettles.

Now comes the process of parching the rice, which, after being put in these large kettles, must be kept moving around and around, much like popcorn. This stirring is done with paddles shorter than those used in the canoe.

All the time Mother was teaching Min di, Wa goosh was instructing us to make buckets that would be sunk in the ground for use in husking the parched rice. This bucket was eighteen inches across the top, eighteen inches deep, and twelve inches at the bottom. A small measure of rice was poured in the bucket. Then Wa goosh told us to put on our moccasins, the ones that Mother had made for this purpose, to dance in the rice. A rail was built over the bucket, so we could hold on to it while we stepped the dance step that thrashed the rice. It took us about ten minutes for each stomping.

Bishiu was taught to do the next step, or second thrashing. This was to remove the coarse husks, which was accomplished by a certain motion of the hands, using a birch-bark basket made for this purpose.

The third thrashing, Mother did. She refused to leave this to any of the children. The rice dust was kept for food and was considered a delicious side dish. Over it could be poured fish broth or any other broth we happened to have.

In the evening we again sat around the fire. We eagerly looked forward to the stories of our work, what we were to do, and how to do it.

One evening Wa goosh said to mother, "Did you bring the fish nets along?"

When she told him that she had, he suggested that he and Min di go out to set them. Then he explained how we must have fish broth to go over the rice cereal. Then we children could taste how good it was. The two of them went to set the nets.

Before daybreak next morning Mother was out and gathered up the nets. When we got up she had the fish boiled and ready for breakfast. And did we enjoy this! We ate until we thought we wouldn't be able to move!

Also we were taught to make dolls and animals from the inner bark of the cedar. These we would stuff with rice, which was one way of preserving our rice.

When at last the time came to break camp, we did not carry back our birch bark and poles. We just broke camp and piled the wigwam bark and containers that were used for the rice in one big pile near a tree and fastened them down with rocks, tied with wegoob. We knew it would be there for us when again we came at the season of the rice harvest.

The first cold breath of the North Wind had come early this year, so we knew what we must expect . . . a long winter. We would have to hasten to get the wood in, before the snows got too deep.

Wa goosh told Mother he would fell a few trees and we boys could saw off the branches and haul all the smaller wood. He would cut and split the larger trees. We made fun of this by making sleds, and on one trip Osh kin played he was a horse, and the next trip I would do the same.

As the days grew shorter and the great snows covered the fields and forests, Wa goosh would come over and shoot ducks and partridges. Then he would put their heads under their wings and freeze them, after which they would be packed in birch-bark baskets and stacked in a makeshift shed.

It was necessary to have abundant rabbit meat for our needs. To bring in the rabbits was always the boy's job. And this made us feel grown up. Mother and Min di would jokingly ask how many we thought we would bring in, as though they wanted to have enough water on for the cooking.

Twin Lakes was now frozen over. It looked like a beautiful great mirror. It also offered great skating, the ice being so smooth that the wind just swept the snow right off to the far shore. There it drifted high.

We "made hay while the days were clear," and when the snow finally covered the ice, we were ready to turn to other games.

One day Wa goosh said, "Way quah, I'm going to show you how to prepare ourselves for the great hunt."

He explained that by this he meant really large game. "You shall help me and see for yourself how it is done," he said. "Tonight I shall hang out the clothes to be worn. They must stay in the night air until ready to be put on."

He built a small wigwam, just large enough to crawl in. After these preparations, he told me I could go to bed and that he would call me in the morning.

I was startled awake while darkness still covered

the white earth when he exclaimed, "Come now, Way quah, I need your help."

So we took three large rocks from the firebed that had been pushed forward till they were red hot. These he piled in the center of the wigwam and then he crawled in, naked.

I was told to stay outside of the wigwam and give him all the water he could drink, in order to clean him out from the inside and also to make him sweat freely.

After about five minutes of this treatment he had me put a large handful of dry cedar needles on the rocks. This essence would go all through his pores, and, with an empty stomach, he would soon be odorless, except for the smell of the cedar trees. After remaining there for about fifteen minutes, he put on fresh clothing and was ready to start on his hunting trip.

Wa goosh explained to me every detail of these preparations. He would not eat anything—just drink water—until after the kill. For if a man went hunting while hungry, he would get his game sooner. The philosophy of this was that there would be more urge than if he went with a full stomach.

He carried enough meal in a little bundle tied to his pack-strap to last two or three days. A pack-strap was a piece of deekskin, tanned with the fur on it. It was about eighteen inches long and some three inches wide. Rawhide fastened on both ends made a tie of four feet. The deerskin was worn over the forehead, then the pack was tied to fall over the small of the back. This was the simplest and easiest way to carry animals, wood or any heavy load to be moved any distance.

The hunting meal was odorless too. It contained parched rice, ground jerky meat, and maple sugar, all mixed together. One man, he said, could travel far or work hard on just one handful of this very tasty food. Being dry, it needed a lot of chewing, and this was supposed to be one reason for Indians having such beautiful teeth.

After Wa goosh started on this trip, I crawled back into bed. He returned that evening just after darkness had settled over the wigwam. Dropping his bundle outside, he entered the wigwam and called for some hot tea. Then he told how he had traveled far into the forest before sighting a deer. Fortunately, he made a kill.

While he drank his tea, Mother left the wigwam and returned with his bundle. We stared at it, for there was a two-year-old buck deer.

Mother soon had it dressed and strung up on a tree.

"How much will you take home?" Mother asked.

"Nothing," Wa goosh replied. "But I will ask that you make for me a pair of moccasins."

In the days that followed, Wa goosh taught us how to make decoys to be used for catching fish through holes in the ice. He built what was called a "dark house," over a hole in the ice. He used a gig, or spear, and by giving the decoy short jerks, it would spin around in the water and attract the fish. In this way we could spear them.

We would then throw them on the ice, and very soon they would be frozen as hard as cordwood sticks.

When we had five or six hundred pounds, they would be taken to town and sold. We always kept enough, of course, for our immediate needs.

Sometimes the winter winds made it almost impossible to remain out of doors, and the snows became very deep on the ground. It was then that we remained in the wigwam, around the fire. But we kept busy making birch-bark baskets and containers to be used later to catch sap from the maple trees. We had to have about a thousand or fifteen hundred of these.

We made little troughs two or three inches wide, cut from the cedar logs. These were about sixteen inches long. We needed as many of these as we had containers. Mother left us making these while she and Min di went to Bagley for supplies.

It was a day's walk from our home to the city. But we had no idea we would be left alone for so long, although we had an abundance of food. Mother evidently knew I could be depended upon to attend to the fires and bring in the wood to keep warm.

During the long absence of Mother and Min di, we kept busy making pretty baskets with the intention of taking them out to sell them when the right time came.

But finally we became quite worried. Peeking outside we saw great flakes coming down and it seemed they would never stop. We fully expected Mother and Min di by nightfall, but at last we could not keep awake any longer and went to sleep.

But with the dawn there was no sign of the absent ones. Bishiu did the cooking with troubled face, and I kept busy with some chores, ever so often looking out to seek for those for whom we waited.

Another night passed with the snow still falling heavily. It covered the earth with a great white blanket.

At the end of the third day, they returned at last. The reason for the long delay had been due to the fact that walking was very difficult and the trails were blanketed with snow. On the way home, about two hours from town, they had come to a little clearing and were trying to decide where they would stay for the night. They remembered a shelter a little farther on and planned to get there before nightfall. But all this time the snow was getting deeper and deeper and drifting with the wind.

They had thrown their packs to the ground to rest, and then, just as they picked them up to move on, they saw something at the edge of the clearing. It was a big timber wolf. For a moment they stood still, frightened. But as the wolf made no move, Mother, who always carried a knife or hatchet, got a piece of birch bark from a nearby tree to use as a torch.

Then Min di secured a club about six feet long and threw it over her shoulder to make the wolf think she had a gun. After lighting the torch, they put on their packs and started out to encircle the beast—but before they got very far into the woods it had disappeared. Then they came back to the road again. The fire and the make-believe gun had saved them from disaster.

"I want this to be a lesson to you children," said Mother. "Remember how useful a tree can be. It protects the animal by giving it shelter and protects us if we know how to use it. The tree gives us bark for almost anything."

Mother and Min di were both exhausted from the journey and the excitement. Bishiu made them some hot tea and soon they were feeling better— but ready for bed.

The next day, Mother inspected the work we had done and nodded her head in approval.

The time came when we began on the strips for the sugar bush house. This is the enclosure where sap from the maple trees is boiled down and made into sugar. Sugar bush is the name given to groups of maple trees—sometimes as many as twenty-five acres—and it is here that the sugar house is built.

This time Mother explained that the house would be a little different—on the order of a square tent. The opening at the top was from one end to the other. The poles that were on each end were about four inches thick and the pole across the top laid in the crotch of the two uprights was the same thickness. This would hold the large kettles used for boiling down the sap.

Mah ni remained at home with the baby until we got everything hauled to the sugar bush. This was located in a deep, dark hardwood forest. The supplies for our work we had to pack on our backs.

Mother made the trails by breaking twigs as she went along, letting them hang in the direction she was going. So she had to start out a half an hour or so ahead of us. But we soon caught up with her and, in our impatience, ran ahead, thinking she was very slow. More than once, however, we found to our surprise that we had gone the wrong way.

Our destination was a good half-day distant. Our loads were heavy. But Mother went as straight as an arrow, never once losing her sense of direction.

We arrived at noon and, as is usual with boys, we were starved. Bishiu prepared some food for us as soon as things were unpacked. Mother looked over the ground carefully and finally selected a place for the construction of the sugar bush house.

The next task was to dig a well. This had to be near the house. Three feet down we found water.

For firewood we had to get hardwood stumps and branches. We worked until we were tired and then asked Mother if we couldn't go home.

"You have worked hard and faithfully," she admitted. "And the darkness comes soon. It is well that we go now."

We rushed through the forest like little deer, toward home. We did not need Mother to show us the trail. We were there long before she arrived and immediately we started gathering wood in our arms and carried it in. By the time Mother had returned we had enough wood for both night and morning.

Mother was pleased. "I'm proud of you, my children," she said, "and the Great Spirit will smile on you."

We were permitted to sit up very late into the night, listening to Mother tell us about the different kinds of sugar cakes we were to get and instruct us as to what we should do the next day.

We were very busy the next day making birchbark molds for these cakes. We designed them in the form of animals: horses, cows, pigs, deer, bear, moose, and even the fowls. They were quite crude, but we were proud of them.

Although we were up with the dawn, it took us all the rest of that day to move the rest of our camping equipment for our sugar bush. We did not need a lot of provision, as we would only be there for three weeks.

It was quite late that night when we returned home, but Mah ni, who had remained in the wigwam with Ahmeek while we moved, had no fear.

The next morning we covered the top opening of the wigwam so if it stormed the water would not do any damage while we were away. The door flap was fastened down with rocks and tied on the sides.

Bishiu started off with Ahmeek on her back. When she got tired, one of us would take him. This relieved the burden, for six miles would have been a long way for one person to carry him. We could not let him walk, as he used his legs very slowly. But we had a lot of fun, and when we boys took him we would run with him, much to his enjoyment.

Mah ni wasn't strong like her brothers and sisters, so all she carried was a sewing basket with her beads and porcupine quills. She always took her beading along, and her little hands were constantly busy.

At night we slept under the stars and could hear the mournful hoot of the great owls, the menacing howls of wolves, and the weird calls of the other night life in the forest.

Mother, Min di, and Bishiu got busy building the sugar bush house while Osh kin and I kept on gathering wood. When it seemed to us that we had enough, Mother set us straight by telling us that we would need much more than that, for the fires must be kept going all day and most of the night. It had to be all hardwood, for the pine knots would make the sugar taste of pitch.

Mah ni sat by the fire and cared for the baby. She was an unusually good little mother and was a great help. Ahmeek was not a great bother, but he did have to have someone to mind him, and he and Mah ni were very happy. Bishiu did most of the cooking while Min di helped Mother with the sugar bush.

It was on the second night that we slept in the sugar bush house. Again we were allowed to stay up late, as Mother instructed us as to what had to be done on the next day. Min di and Bishiu tested the baskets to see they did not leak. This was done by setting them in a larger container filled with water. If they passed the test they were sent out and were ready for the tapping.

It was now time for the heavy snows to melt. Soon, O-pee-chee, the robin, would come from his home in the South to announce the Spring. The sun shone down bright and warm on the white earth, so that during the day the underfooting was wet and slippery. At night it would grow cold again and the slush would freeze. It was this freezing and thawing that started the sap to flow from the maple trees.

All of this I was learning during my very first experience helping with the sugar-making.

Mother did the tree-tapping, which was a job that required skill. With two strokes of the axe she would have the sap running, and at the third stroke she put in the trough.

We remained right behind her to set the basket underneath in order to catch the very first precious drops. Without any lost motion Mother was at the next tree, and we were forced to keep up with her.

It all depended on the size of the tree how many taps she put into the trunk. Usually it took from three to seven, and she could make as many as five hundred taps in a day. She had the reputation of being the best tapper in that part of the country. And she always knew that her axe must never harm the tree itself.

The person tapping trees in a given area of ground were considered to have that area for their own, but only for the sugar bush. But no other Indian would trespass on this domain.

One morning, soon after we had started tapping the trees for the sugar water, Wa goosh came up to us.

"I paid a visit to your wigwam," he told us, "to

37

see Min di, but found the door closed. Knowing it was sugar bush time, I followed your trail here."

"It is good to have you come, Wa goosh," said Mother.

"And I hope I have come in time to help with the making of sugar," said Wa goosh, as he noticed our sugar bush house and the many baskets for the bringing of the sap. "But I must tell you that I have never learned the ways of sugar-making."

"Then Dekaince will teach you," my mother said with a smile. "Come with me."

Mother demonstrated the tapping, and it seemed very easy. Then she handed him the axe.

"Now you try it," she said encouragingly.

Wa goosh took the axe with confidence, but he soon learned that it was much more difficult than he anticipated. It took a great deal of practice to hit the tree at the right angle and do it so that only three or four strokes were needed.

The night Mother told Osh kin and me that with another day we would have a different job. We must bring in the sap and pour it into the barrels. Now, for once, we would have all the sap we could drink.

When we said this, Mother just smiled, for well she knew that we would have our fill long before we would really do any work.

With the first gleam of the sun through the trees, we were out with our buckets, going from tree to tree, tasting of each one, seeing which had the best sap.

When I would find a very sweet one, I would call

over to Osh kin. And if he found one, he would call me.

We did not work much in the early part of the day, but by noon, nevertheless, the three barrels were getting full. But the sap was still dripping fast.

We looked at Mother pleadingly. "May we have a rest now?" we asked.

She shook her head. "No, my children, you must make the fires under the kettles. For now it is time to start boiling for the syrup."

This task of boiling the sap was turned over to Min di. It was no light responsibility, as there were three very large kettles hung side by side over the fire pit. It was not long before the barrels were empty and we had to go once again for more sap. It was not so easy this time, as the nearby trees had been taken care of first. It required longer to walk back and forth.

It was not too long, however, before we had them filled again. When we told Mother that we had finished, she called to Min di to take some larger baskets of birch bark for temporary use, for as soon as it was too dark to tap any more, she would boil it down faster than it would run.

Thus we worked far into the night.

At noon the next day, when Mother had finished tapping the trees that had been marked off, it was interesting to see that the boiling sap was turning into rich heavy syrup. Sister did the testing, being careful to see that the syrup was ready to put into the molds.

We worked all that day like beavers, and Min di said, "When night falls, Mother will finish her work and we will put the syrup in the molds."

We looked forward most eagerly to this and wondered how the molds would turn out.

Later on, we were careful to place the molds where they would cool quickly. As soon as we got what we wanted, the rest was beaten until it powdered into sugar. This was brought about through continual stirring after the kettles had been taken off the direct heat.

The sugar, thus powdered, was put into containers that had been specially made for the purpose. They were sewed up and could be preserved for several winters if not needed at once.

Mother had made about one hundred pounds of sugar and nearly as much in weight of sugar cakes. And on top of that there were gallons of maple syrup. It meant that she would have had even more, had we children not planted sugar cakes in the snow for future eating. But she did not scold us for this.

Wa goosh had already returned to his own wigwam, but by the time we were ready to leave our sugar bush for home, he returned to the camp. As was his nature, he was most helpful, and he assisted in hauling the sugar and supplies back. This made the load much easier for all of us.

Home looked good to us, despite all of the fun we had enjoyed at the sugar bush. It seemed that the trees had taken on new dresses of green and here and there we could see a tree that was a little different from the rest—covered with beautifully colored blossoms.

The squirrels were a little more bold than usual and came scampering around us, as if to say, "Catch us if you can—but you'll have to put down your load if you do." And so we did lay down our loads and chase them—but just for the fun of seeing them go for the trees. We could not catch them . . . and how they would scold!

Finally, when we emerged from the forest trail and walked along the shores of the lake, we welcomed the sight of our wigwam in the distance. And so ended our adventure until the next sugar making.

CHAPTER V

SUMMERTIME again! The warm smile of the sun had melted almost the very last of the heavy winter snows—all except little patches of white that lay here and there in the deepest shadows of the forest.

The robin had already perched himself in trees wherever there was a ray of sunlight, and in pine and oak and birch that surrounded our wigwam. Here he sang his joyous song of welcome. He seemed to know that no harm would come to him at the hand of any Indian, that no arrow would fly from strung bow or loaded gun to take away his little life.

Now once more it was time of Segum, the Spring, that period bordering on Summer. But we liked to think it was already Summer, although the Spring was possibly the most beautiful time of the year.

No longer did the frost come when the sun started on its journey over the night sky trail. No longer did the sap flow from the sugar bush. Lakes were filled from the melting snows and the earth was full of the waters that would bring about abundant crops during the growing season that was to come. New life was swelling the buds on fruit-bearing trees and bush and vine.

Here and there was a tinge of green as new grass showed its tender shoots through the brown earth that had for so long lain as dead. And there was the pale green rice-grass that fringed the shores of the many lakes. Violets poked their heads through pine needles and leaves that carpeted the floor of the forest adding great beauty with their bright colors to the velvet-like mosses.

Mother had busied herself with the cleaning out of the storage pit and took the potatoes that were left out of doors. And now she required more space for the syrup and sugar.

She paused for a spell in her work as Osh kin and I came up to the wigwam after a trip into the forest. We realized that the birch supply was getting low. We wanted to surprise Mother by bringing back some bark.

This was the time when bark stripping was at its best. How proud we were when we threw down our bundles, just like we had seen the older ones do.

Mother could not hide the look of pride in her eyes as she surveyed the bundles.

"Far into the forest you must have gone to bring this home," she said.

"Yes, Mother," I replied. "We had been following the trail of a deer when we came upon this place."

"Then is there not more like it?" she asked.

"Oh, yes," I told her. "There is plenty for a canoe . . . for there are many trees."

"That is good, my son. Min di and I will return with you on a day very soon. We will have our own canoe—for now you are old enough, as you have proved, to help with the stripping and gathering."

How pleased we were! And it was just a few mornings later that the four of us were on our way. Along the forest trail we trudged, following the path that was already familiar to us boys.

For some reason I had never before been so alert to the voices of the forest. The murmur of pine, fir, and hemlock seemed to caress my ears. And then there was the soft cooing of wood doves, the hoot of the owl and the whirring of wings as birds flitted from tree to tree, from branch to branch.

I loved the crunch of fern and pine needles beneath my feet. The forest seemed to welcome me to her damp, verdant bosom and to the great silence of these shadowy places where the Indian or white man so seldom came.

We breathed deeply of the fragrance and at times were far in the lead of Mother and Min di. But we knew they would have no trouble following our trail.

During the journey, Mother had been looking for roots and tasting and digging up different kinds.

I stopped and went over to her. "Why do you

43

search for these roots, Mother?" I inquired. I was in a hurry to arrive at the grove of trees, our rendezvous.

But Mother remained silent and went right on with her search.

Finally we arrived at the end of our quest and proudly we pointed out the trees where the birch bark was fine and well suited for the making of our canoe . . . our canoe that later on we would launch on the smooth waters of the nearby lake. We would paddle it perhaps to the distant shore, where new mysteries might seem to be lurking.

Mother now pointed out the trees that would supply the longest and widest strips of bark. So while we boys did the stripping, she and Min di cleaned off the bark.

Thus we worked until Mother said it was enough for our boat and other immediate needs.

It was quite a load to pack home, however. On our way we stopped at the spot where Mother had placed a dead branch against a tree.

"Why do we stop here?" I demanded, as Mother put down the pack and I did the same—for it was heavy and I was glad to use the pause for a little rest.

"I'm looking for a root that is good for medicine," she answered. "That was the reason I stopped on the way to the grove."

"But why do we need medicine?" I asked. "Is not the Great Spirit able to heal our sickness?"

"It is true, my son—the medicine of the Great Spirit is good. But now Ahmeek has been taken with a sickness that is very great, and the Great

Spirit has not healed him. It may be that we have not listened well to his voice. Sometimes, my son, we depart from the ways of His teachings—and then it is that the sickness and troubles that disturb us come upon our people."

I had gone to the church of the white man, so now it was sometimes hard to understand all she said about the "Great Spirit." The Chippewas heard the voice of God in the whispering of the pines and saw His smile in the rippling waters of the lake, or felt his displeasure in the sudden storm that swayed the tall trees and stirred up great waves on lake and river.

But in the white man's church I had learned much that was different from that of my mother's belief. And so it was all very confusing to me and I did not attempt to straighten it out. The fact was that little brother had been taken with a great sickness and Mother was gathering these healing herbs so that he might get well. That was enough for me to understand at the moment. But I did question Min di when Mother would tell me no more. And to my questions she replied.

"Did you not know that Ahmeek was very sick?"

"I only know that he has no longer the smile that he once had as he looked up at me from his cradle," I said. But I was suddenly very sober and troubled in my heart.

Min di did not speak more about Ahmeek, but went on, "You will have to remember where that root is, for the time may come when you will have to return for more."

So I listened carefully to all that Mother said about this healing root and marked well the place that it grew in the forest . . . places where the shadows were deep.

No longer now did we play in the little clearing where our wigwam stood. Mother told us that on account of Ahmeek we must go down to the lake shore where our voices would not disturb brother.

Mother went about her work most soberly. It was plain that her heart was heavy.

And then the day came when we were sent to the forest for more of the herbs. When we returned I entered the wigwam. There sat Mother beside Ahmeek. She was crooning a lullaby that I had often heard before. But now her voice was different as she sang in a monotone, "Wah . . . wah . . . wah." It was not the lullaby that would croon little brother to sleep—for she had said it was not well for him to sleep so much and to give no heed to what was going on about him.

As I stood beside Mother looking down upon the pale, thin face of little Ahmeek, I missed the happy smile he had until lately flashed upon me. He just lay there, very quietly . . . only once in a while a whimper would issue forth from his thin little lips. It was plain that the shadow of Pan Guk hovered near.

I went from the wigwam and moved slowly on downward to the lake. The birds seemed to be singing as cheerily as ever and the sun was shining with its usual radiance on the peaceful lake . . . but it was not the same now with me. My own heart, like that of Mother's was heavy with a dread of what might come. But I could not understand how the Great Spirit, who was the Giver of all life and happiness, could have departed from our wigwam. I could not fathom how the death spirit could have entered to take his place. Until then I had seen no sickness. I was very much perplexed indeed.

There came a time soon after this day when I looked upon the suffering form of Ahmeek, the day when Mother crooned her sad lullaby, that I was engaged in the hauling of wood. It was the time of day when the shadows from the surrounding trees were long and soon the night would come.

Mother stopped me as I went from the wigwam to procure another load.

"Way quah," she said, "Ahmeek no longer takes his food, and the medicine I gave to him he only gives up again. I fear that he has not much longer to stay with us. Will you go for Raven Feather?"

Raven Feather was the Indian who had been taught the ways of the white man and was now a preacher to the Chippewas. We had often walked to the church and well did I know the trail. I ran all the way to the home of this man who taught us to worship the white man's God. At my knock the door opened and there stood an Indian as stalwart and straight as the pine tree. As he looked at me from kindly brown eyes and smiled pleasantly, I stood timidly trying to give him my message.

"Way quah gishig!" he exclaimed after a moment. "What is it that brings you here?" He saw that I was still breathing hard from my running.

"My brother Ahmeek, who was taken with a strange sickness, no longer smiles when we play with him. Mother says that you, Raven Feather, should come at once. Death may even now arrive before you get there." I talked to him in the language of the Indian and knew he would understand even though he now had taken to the ways of the white man and worshipped their God.

"Raven Feather will go at once," he promised.

I darted off. By several short cuts I made three miles back so quickly that Min di wouldn't at first believe I had actually made the trip there and back.

The preacher came just a few minutes later. But already the death spirit hovered very closely to the now still form of little Ahmeek. It was just a little while later that the death angel took my brother from us. Then it was that Raven Feather prayed for this one who had departed never to return . . . prayed that his spirit, as he named it, would be happy in heaven where one as innocent and pure as little Ahmeek would surely go.

On the next day, Raven Feather returned to our wigwam again. At this time there was a prayer meeting and the Indians had gathered for the last rites. They sang hymns and visited till daylight. One of the songs they sang was "Lead Kindly Light," which in Chippewa tongue goes as follows:

Lead kindly light, amid the encircling gloom.
1. *Man o su dush, kin Wayaseyaziyun,*
    Sagin kenshin!
    Kush kid'bikut, waso go endyean,
    Sagin kenshin!
    Wijiwishin! Api iu majayan
    Iu wasa eyag; Jiwabudaman.

2. *Kichi kinwenj, kawin nigi nendazi*
    Jiwi-jiwyun;
    Nogom su dush wijisishin; gaye
    Sagin kenshin!
    Nigisegis su, kibataziyan,
    Mano su kin, abueyenimishin.

3. *Meshkawaiziyun, mano su geyabi*
    Sagin kenshin!
    Sanagut su, wanijayan nananj
    Ishgua 'bikuk;
    Kakijeb su ang'nug ta mojgis -wug,
    Api wijiwagua, kasag-agig.

Wa goosh asked a neighbor to assist in making the coffin. When it was finished, Min di lined the little box with white satin and covered the outside with black satin.

But the beauty of this coffin that held the still white form of the one I loved could not make me forget my grief. Our friends went into the woods to gather wild flowers, while others brought them by the bunch.

On the next day the little coffin was put in a light

49

wagon and taken to the church of Raven Feather.

It was all like a horrible dream to Osh kin and me. Never before had we seen anything like it. And it was many days before I could go about my work and play as once I had done.

CHAPTER VI

THE VISITS OF Wa goosh were something we looked forward to with delight, although we knew that he came mostly to see Min di. He and sister would go out walking together.

But Wa goosh always had something new to teach us. We thus learned about the different kinds of barks, roots, and herbs. He and Min di, on returning from their strolls in the woods, would bring all kinds of roots, chips, leaves, and grasses.

"Why," I asked at one time, "do you gather all of this?" And Min di answered for them both.

"When you are older," she said, "you will want to learn all about these same leaves and roots. But now you are young. You would not so easily understand."

With those many trips Wa goosh made to visit Sister, together with the times we boys had gone to his home, the trail became well tramped. So now it was easy enough to find our way. One day Wa goosh came again.

"I have come," he explained, "to tell you that the prices for snake root are going to be high. If you can find and dig them, I will get my team and wagon and help."

"We will go," Mother assured him. "But I shall need time."

Already Wa goosh had made hoes for Mother and Min di, and now he made one for each of us boys. It was a special kind of hoe, made just to dig out the dirt from around the roots.

Wa goosh's people had so many kinds of machinery that they could do almost anything—such as mending racks, plows or tools. They could shoe horses, too. I had often visited over there in order to learn so many things that were strange to me.

And so it was that in a few days we were ready to go again into the deep forest to dig the snake root.

It was not long before we had Wa goosh's wagon loaded down and were on our way. Mother rode in front with Min di and Wa goosh. They were trying to decide where was the best place to go.

"Would you care to go to camp on Roy Lake?" Wa goosh suggested.

"Yes," nodded Mother, who seemed to know all about those things. "But I will get off at the spot where this root is best. You and the girls can go and make camp. The boys will remain with me, if they wish."

It was still early Spring, so the snake root was not yet in blossom. But at last we stopped at the place where Mother said the gathering would be best. Here we took our hoes and sacks from the wagon and waited for further instructions.

"Here," said Mother, "is one of the roots. Look at it. See how it grows. Notice the shape of its leaves. They are long and pointed—something like the grass that grows by the lakes. To dig them out you hit down with your hoe, then give a little jerk. Next grab the grass and pull. You will find it is much like an octopus. Now hit the roots against the hoe and the dirt will fall away. Break off the green tops and put the roots in your sack."

Soon my brother and I were bragging over our speed in pulling the snake root. It was a contest as to who would get the biggest root for his sack. More than once we were badly fooled, for the ones with the most growth above the ground had the smallest roots.

For a time the work was, in our estimation, real fun, but soon we were tired. And then, too, we got very hungry. Finally we returned to where the others had made camp. Here dinner was served to us.

The four who had already gone on ahead had pitched the main tent. Into this they had unloaded our bedding and food. Inasmuch as this was the time for the big rains we had to be prepared for the unexpected storms.

After the feast, Osh kin and I gathered up some cedar boughs for our beds. We cut poles on which to hang three mosquito bars. Later in the evening these would be erected. But now we wanted to play. So we climbed trees and made a game of striving for the highest perch that would allow the greatest vision of the forest growth.

Min di and Wa goosh left us to go for a walk together. It was almost dark before they returned, but
they sat down and told us of the beautiful waterfall
they had visited near the lake and how they enjoyed
the beauty that was all about them. Across the lake
they had seen a dense swamp where the grasses were
all green along the shoreline.

They told how a big buck had come out of the bog
and stood there, alert and ready to dart back into
the blackness of the trees at the first sign that he
had been discovered. But Wa goosh had taken no
gun, so the buck was in no danger. For it seemed
that Wa goosh had been thinking only of being
alone with Min di.

Meanwhile Brother and I had been racing up
and down the beach. Here we discovered an old
homemade boat, hidden far back in the brush.

We took Wa goosh to the spot and showed him
our find.

"This is good," he said enthusiastically. "You
did well. And now if you will keep away from the
lake tomorrow, I'm sure the deer about which I
told you will come back in the evening time. Then
Min di and I will use this boat to go after him."

All the next day we worked hard at digging snake
root. But the time dragged along. It seemed so slow
before the sun had made its way across the blue
sky to hide finally behind the tall trees! For
we were looking forward with the keenest interest
in the deer hunt. Wa goosh was a very brave hunter.
Most surely we would have venison on this trip.

At last the great moment came. Wa goosh arrived

with his gun. And again he and Min di went off together. But this time, as we well knew, it was not just to be in each other's company. They got into the boat we had found and shoved off toward the opposite shore.

We boys could not go along, for we might do something that would scare the deer away. So we climbed one of the trees by the shore of the lake and from there we would have a splendid view of all that went on.

Soon we saw them paddling around the shore of the lake. We could hear them talking in low tones and their paddles hardly caused a ripple in the smooth surface of the water.

The sun was low in the western sky. There were long shadows cast by the trees near the lake shore. The sky was a golden glow as the sun reflected against some clouds just over the tree tops.

All was peaceful and quiet. The boat bearing Sister and Wa goosh glided as silently as a swan over the water. But suddenly they came to a stop not far from the spot where the buck had shown himself the evening before.

Would he come again, as Wa goosh had said? Or would he remain in the safety of the forest as deer sometimes did, looking out from the dense growth with suspicious eyes and then dashing back into the shadows?

Although it seemed like a long, long time, we really didn't have long to wait. The setting sun still hovered in the western sky before it dipped down to start its journey over the night sky trail. Its rays still tinted the fast-greying clouds and reflected it-self in the tops of the surrounding trees.

Then the moment for which we had so excitedly waited arrived. The deer appeared at the edge of the trees. It stood there a long minute, looking cautiously out. Then it slowly ventured out onto the bog that lay between the forest and the lake shore. There it was, the same golden color that Wa goosh and Min di had told us about the evening before.

We boys, still sitting in the tree and holding our breath, knew that the others in the boat were probably just as anxious as we were.

Slowly Wa goosh raised his gun and aimed. There was a loud report, the sound echoing and re-echoing from shore to shore. The buck gave three leaps, or sort of jerky jumps, and then he fell to his knees.

The deer remained in that position for a moment, as if saying a prayer to the Great Spirit. Then it sank slowly to the ground, rolling over on its side and lay still.

We almost felt sorry that so splendid an animal should have to die by the hand of the hunter.

Wa goosh and Sister were out of the boat immediately and after the deer almost before it died. They bled him at once, then loaded him into the boat and rowed back to the shore where we were waiting. We had our knives ready to help with the skinning, but Mother pushed us aside.

"This I will do myself," she ordered. "I want it whole, and it is not well to use a knife except for slitting the legs and belly."

Soon the buck was skinned and the body, still warm, was hung from a limb well out of reach of prowling wolves and other animals that might scent the fresh meat and come to help themselves.

It was well after the time when darkness had settled over the woods. Birds had already gone to their rest. The moon had started its path across the night sky to follow the sun that had gone down on the opposite horizon. A lone animal called to its mate in the distance, but there was no answering call; nothing but the eerie hoot of an owl close by our wigwam, where a fire burned brightly to cook the evening meal and to drive away the chill which always came with night at this time of the year.

Soon the fire died down to its glowing embers. We all made ready our beds on either side of the firepit, and while the dull embers still sent their smoke lazily upwards and out through the opening above, we lay down for a well-earned rest. The sleep spirit crooned a lullaby that made our eyes heavy and we slept.

I dreamed of brave hunters and daring deeds with arrow and gun. I had grown to a young brave and much venison and bear meat did I bring home to our wigwam. I was swift of foot and could outdistance most animals of the wild. I had learned well the ways of the forest and the many animals that roamed there, and I was not afraid.

And then there came another vision—one that made me a bit sad. It was of a beautiful buck deer, soft of eye and swift of foot, standing at the edge of the woods looking across the lake. It was as if it were standing looking over at the wigwam and lodge of the Indian, not wanting to be afraid and longing for the friendship of those whose arrows were sharp and swift, and whose thunder sticks sometimes crippled or killed. In my sleep I saw again that buck deer that had sunk to its knees and remained that way a moment as in prayer.

We arose with the dawn and helped to prepare the now cold deer and make it into "jerky." We boys made our own rack and helped to cut up the meat. Mother then took the hide to get it ready for tanning. First she placed it in a boiler, covering it over with water and then sprinkling hardwood ashes over all. This was left thus for two days in order to remove the hide.

The deer skin was then put on a log that had been peeled for the purpose until it was very smooth. Mother used a scraper on both sides to re-move all the hair on the outside and fatty substance inside.

It was hard work and took all of our patience, for it was necessary that the hide be not roughened or cut—otherwise it would be of no value for the various needs to which it would be put.

Next came the washing and rinsing job; then wrapping it around two sticks, one at either end. The skin was twisted and twisted until it was wrung out dry.

We boys would sit facing each other, feet to feet to better brace ourselves. Then we pulled and turned until the skin was thoroughly stretched and perfectly dry. Mother would come over to us ever so often and examine the results of our efforts. If the skin was still stiff and hard, she would put it through the washing process and we would do the stretching and twisting all over again.

At last the job was finished. Mother had prepared a mixture composed of water and the brains of the deer. Into this she put the skin, explaining it was to soften the hide. There it remained for two more days while the water and brains mixture did its curing work.

We stretched the hide on a framework of upright sticks, again using the scraper on both sides. Again it was taken from the frame and once more stretched by hand. Now we could see that the skin was perfectly white, as Mother explained it should be.

Now came the tanning to the desired shade. To accomplish this it was sewed very loosely together, something like a pocket, and hung up over a hardwood fire that had been burned down to live coals over which dried pine cones or willow twigs were placed to make the required smoke. The hide was draped around the fire much like a tent, and we had to watch it very closely to make sure that no flame touched the precious hide.

When at last we had thus secured the desired shade, the hide was turned inside out and again draped around the fire, until that side also was just the right tan. And now it was ready for use . . . that hide that just a few days before had covered the throbbing, warm body of a beautiful buck deer. One such hide would make four good pairs of moccasins, and the rest could be used for beaded bags or strings that were needed for different purposes.

I had already learned there were several kinds of moccasins, according to the uses they would be put. There were moccasins for the girls and women. They were higher and tied about the ankles tightly, were plain and made of buck skin.

The moccasins for men and boys were low cut— more like slippers—and were also plain for everyday use. Then there were dress moccasins, for both men and women. These were elaborately beaded, having a beaded band about three inches wide. The beads were in colored leaf, buds, or small flowers and vines. On the instep was a bud or flower.

Mah ni it was who did most of the bead work. She wasn't as strong and sturdy as most Indian maidens, so she did not go into the woods too often, or over the lakes when the rice was ready for gathering. So she had much time to sew. She did some of the bead work on velvet, sewing it onto our moccasins. This made them very pretty. How I loved to watch her as she sat there making the various designs! I was much interested in the beading, and as often as the opportunity presented itself I would do some also.

The Indian belief had always been that the father would get the heaviest part of the hide for his moccasins. But having no father with us, I was considered the head of the household, although only a boy. So I was very proud to get the best pair. It was quite an occasion for us all to wear new moccasins.

When we brought the snake root to camp, we laid it out in the sun. If we had a good warm, balmy day it would dry within a few hours. After it was thoroughly dry, we piled it up. One time when Wa goosh came, he saw we had quite a supply of snake root. He suggested to Mother that he would take it to town for her. She had been relying on him to do this for her—so she was glad for his offer.

Min di went with him and Mother asked Mah ni if she wanted to send some of her work, too. When I heard this I was fearful they would take my moccasins, so I tried to hide them. Mother had a good laugh and promised she wouldn't take them from me, because one of these days, she said, very soon, we would all be going into town. Then I could wear them and show them off.

With their return home from town they brought a goodly supply of groceries, for which they had exchanged the snake root.

We were very anxious to see what they had brought. Like children, we were sure they brought us something nice. We didn't crave candies or sweets because we always had hard maple candy. So if it were only a loaf of bread, that would be a wonderful treat.

And they did bring us some! After that we dug snake root every day, making several trips to town with it—so we always had a good supply of edibles.

At that season, strawberries were very plentiful and ripe. We would hunt out a good patch and then Mother would call to Wa goosh and we would all go berry picking. We discovered that the raspberries were ripe also and later we went back to pick them.

It was lots of fun, and after eating all we wanted there were still many containers full.

These birch-bark containers were made as needed. We didn't have to carry them along with us.

Mother had much fruit to can now. We had plenty of groceries and would have a big supply of strawberry sauce too. She made the sauce for the strawberries and other fruits with a mixture of maple sugar. The canned berries were sealed in old brown jugs. The sealing was done with pitch, which was made from balsam and white pine. It never hardened. Then the jugs were stored away in the food pits that we had for that purpose in the wigwam.

Besides strawberries, we picked choke-cherries, black haws, blueberries and the high bush cranberries. These too were canned by Mother.

CHAPTER VII

THE Morrison family, Betow and Nig nah qwah om oquay, who brought Osh kin home, often visited us. When they came they would bring Osh kin something new—clothes, shoes or anything he happened to say he liked. As time went on, I noticed how they thus favored him. I noticed, too, at these times he would draw away from me. Was he ashamed, I wondered, that I wasn't getting things also? Or was it that he feared I might! I couldn't figure it out, but anyway Bishiu and I began more and more to turn to each other. She was such a comfort to me. So as Osh kin drew away, she became ever closer.

One day Mother said to Min di, "Ask Way quah what he thinks about Osh kin going with Betow and his wife. They want to adopt him." Mother was having a hard time keeping us all, and she thought that maybe Brother would have a better home with them.

Mr. Morrison, Betow (meaning "just a name"), was tall and strong as the pine. He had a white man's hair cut and his brown eyes were always pleasant and smiling. He liked children, but especially Osh kin.

Mrs. Morrison, Nigah nah qwah om oquay (meaning "leader thunder woman"), was also tall and sturdy. Her hair was straight and black and she wore it in one braid. Her large, long face was pleasant, and her eyes seemed to smile as she showed her strong white teeth. Always was she willing to give a helping hand. She wore a calico dress, tight waisted and full of skirt. She wore earrings and had beads around her neck. She liked Osh kin very much, and it was finally decided to let him go with them just to see if he liked it well enough to remain with them always.

Another misfortune came upon us. My little Sister Mah ni became stricken with a strange illness. It got so she could no longer talk so we could understand and she became very weak. She could not even sit up. To our question, "Why?" Mother and Min di could only look very sad and not attempt to explain as they had during the last sickness of little brother Ahmeek.

It was for that reason Mother seemed glad when Wa goosh trusted me with his canoe. I would take it out on the lake either alone or with Bishiu. Occasionally we would go clear across the lake and visit some of the other Indian children who also had been away to the white man's school. Sometimes this visit would last for several days, and I guess our absence was a relief to Mother as she was bowed down with the burden of Mah ni.

Raven Feather, the preacher, came more than once and often did he offer prayer to the God of the white man for Mah ni. At times others would come and join him in these prayer meetings.

Then came a day when, upon our return home Bishiu and I saw a crowd gathered around our wigwam. They had come in wagons. Horses were staked out to graze or were tied to the hitching rack nearby at the edge of the small clearing. These people were to remain for the night. Everywhere there was a spirit of sadness. Even the trees whispered the message and I knew now for sure that Pan Guk had come to stay until he could take Mah ni with him to the land of shadows over the long sky trail.

Thus it was that death had twice entered our wigwam within this short space of time; and again I wondered why.

Raven Feather buried my sister as he had buried my brother Ahmeek. And they made a coffin much like that of Brother's. They placed the coffin along side his grave under a great sheltering oak tree. It was some comfort to see how the tree's arms spread themselves protectingly over the mounds of earth. There were many flowers now as the summer was well advanced and the days of the warm sun brought new life to all growing things.

Mother rode home with Wa goosh and Min di, but Bishiu and I went off, hand in hand, through the woods towards the home that would now seem empty indeed. As we came out of the woods, to the lake shore, we lingered by the water, tossing stones and talking. Presently Bishiu said, "Way quah, if Git-che-man-itu, Master of Life, takes me before you, I will always be with you. Always remember that."

"Yes, Bishiu," I answered, "and if I am taken first, I will always protect you. No matter where we go or what we do, we will be beside each other."

After this we were never far apart. Whatever the one did the other helped, whether carrying wood, mending shoes or repairing our clothing.

One day the whole family went to visit Osh kin in Wa goosh's wagon. We arrived at the time of the noon meal and they invited us to eat. This is the first thing an Indian does—insist that you feast with him.

But everything was so different—so unlike our wigwam. For they lived in a house. It had three rooms—a downstairs bedroom, a kitchen and a living room. And in the attic was another bedroom. There was a large porch across the front of the house. This overlooked Island Lake. There was a back entrance, but no running water or indoor toilet.

Osh kin slept in the attic bedroom, and he was very anxious to show us his playthings. Bishiu and I noticed a swing. This was something new to us and we ran towards it. It helped to make us forget the gloom that death had brought upon us.

Min di had gone to school with Nigah nah qwah om quay's daughter, Maria, Shing obe (meaning "evergreens"). Shing obe was now married to Sahn sway, and they lived next door to her mother. So Min di and Wa goosh went over to their wigwam. They had to go down a small hill to a plateau, which was about a hundred yards from Nigah nah's modern home.

Nigah nah and Mother were about the same age. They talked together and planned to go over and visit the medicine man.

The folks were still sitting outside and planning all this, when Nigah nah went to the railing of the porch and called to her daughter to tell of these plans. Sahn sway and Wa goosh had come out and were standing on the lake bluff. Their house and wigwam were high up on a bluff about fifty feet above the shore, so they had a nice view. It was now about four o'clock in the afternoon and already the forest shadows were long. Within the trees it was getting very dark.

As the men stood there they saw something moving. They watched it closely. It was going into the

lake from the east shore. Betow came over to them
and they tried to make it out. It couldn't be a horse
or a human being. It was too large for a deer.

For five or ten minutes they continued to watch.
Now it was coming out from the rushes and into the
open lake, heading towards the west shore where
there was a heavy hardwood forest.

"Why don't you two young men go after him?"
Betow suggested. "It's a bear."

They got their canoe and guns in short order and
were off. We three, Bishiu, Osh kin, and I, heard
them and were soon down by the edge of the bluff
where we could see every stroke of the paddles.
What a pretty sight to see the men really paddling
after that bear! They had to head him off, so he
would turn to the little island in the lake. They
first, however, wanted to tire him out, so he wouldn't
fight back too hard.

They knew it would not do to shoot the bear out
in deep water, as a bear when shot dives to the bottom and grabs onto something and there he stays.
They didn't want to lose him. So they drove him
till they could see the bottom of the lake near this
island and then shot him.

The bear dove down as expected, but they threw
a line with an iron hook on it. This snagged their
prey and they pulled him to the surface. Then they
dragged him to the shore and loaded him into the
canoe.

We had a bird's-eye view, and it was an exciting
sight. I had been told about bear meat—how good
it was—but this was to be my first taste.

They skinned the bear and Mother was to tan the hide. Sahn sway paid her to tan it for him. Our trip was well worthwhile, with the hide tanning and the bear meat they gave us to take home.

While the bear was being dressed by the men, Mother and Min di walked over to the medicine man and his wife to invite them for Nigah nah to a bear dinner.

Everyone enjoyed a very delicious feast. Afterwards each of us was given some of the meat to take home.

Way cha ni, the medicine man (meaning "noisy feather"), wore long hair in two braids. He had piercing brown eyes. His dark blue shirt was made of broadcloth, open at the throat, and his dark trousers were held up by a long braided belt. This was made of colored yarn braided together. It was about nine feet long and wrapped around him twice and tied in sash fashion on the side. He always carried his little canvas bag, which held his tobacco and pipe. He also wore a wide-brimmed hat and high shoes.

His wife, Day dah gwah sh quay, was short, heavy set, middle-aged, and very good looking. Her eyes were brown and motherly, and her hair was long and black. She wore a plain dress with a flowered band around the bottom. The sleeves hung loose, and these had cuffs of the same kind of material. She wore beads, earrings and beaded wrist band, and a wide gold ring. On her feet were pretty moccasins.

As it was getting late, we all stayed at Betow's

place. Wa goosh put up the horses in Betow's barn, and we had the experience of sleeping in the house.

Osh kin asked me to stay with him. Min di and Mother made a bed downstairs for Bishiu. Wa goosh prepared a bed for himself up in our room.

On the next morning, we played around until noon, and then Wa goosh loaded into the wagon our bear meat and hide and we started home.

When we finally arrived home, Wa goosh took some meat for his mother and went on his way. It was very late.

CHAPTER VIII

A S WE HAD MISSED school during the year, the authorities looked us up and sent Indian policemen to see that we didn't stay out another year. We had the choice of two schools: White Earth or Beaulieu.

We chose White Earth because we knew some of the other children were going there. Mother said she would let us go, but she needed us to help her get the wild rice in.

We went with her to gather the rice. We wanted some to take to school. It was so good re-parched, even better than candy.

When we got through we made preparations to go to school. While playing we were constantly on the alert for the wagon that would pick us up. The school was about thirty-five miles from home. Now we would return to the use of our English names!

They picked us up first, because we were the farthest away from the school. They drove on around the lake, gathering up other children. Joe Bush, who lived across the lake, centered his attention on me and we soon became friends.

Bishiu and I were the only ones from our home to go, as Min di had graduated the year we came from Flandeau.

Joe told me all about the school, which he had attended the previous year. He knew all of the boys. He said there were two who were considered big bullies. They were about my age and he asked if I knew them. I didn't, but I would very soon. Their names were Wau pee and Ne keek. These boys had older brothers at the school, and that made them think they could run all over the smaller boys. Since Bishiu and I were all alone in the school, they picked on us.

When we arrived, quite a crowd of children had come already, and, as usual, the new boys were soon picked out. One little fellow came up to me.

"Do you know Wau pee and Ne keek?" he asked.

Of course I had been told about their bullying but waited to hear what he would say.

"Well," he went on, "they are about your size. Do you think you could whip them?"

"I don't know," I replied. "I hadn't planned on having to fight. I came here to learn something."

Just then we were ordered to go to the commissary for our uniforms and clothing, and nothing more was said on the matter. But one day as I came through the door from the school room, this Wau pee bumped into me.

"Watch where you're going, won't you!" he growled. It was plain he was trying to pick a fight. The other boys were of course always looking for a good scrap. Even the larger ones tried to encourage a fight. We went from the building to the grounds and they kept at me, starting to call me a coward. I didn't want to fight, but I couldn't let them call me a name like that. The bigger boys said, "Wait till you get to the basement of the boys' building. Then you can have it out there."

Some of them put chips of bark on the shoulder of each of us. Wau pee came over and knocked mine off. I reached over and knocked his off, and the fight was on. It lasted about four or five minutes. I knocked him down and grabbing him by the shoulders pulled him to his feet again.

"Do you want some more?" I asked.

"No," he cried, "don't hit me again!" He put an arm over his face for protection. I pushed it down again and said:

"Do you still want to fight me?" But he admitted he had had enough. He had a black eye and his mouth was swollen. I wasn't even scratched. So I had beaten him.

I had the name now of being the first one who could beat him, and all the boys were for me. Ne keek wasn't around to see what had happened, so some of the boys asked me:

"Do you think you could whip Ne keek, seeing Wau pee was so easy for you?"

"Maybe I could," I told them, "but I don't want to fight. But I'm not afraid of anyone my own size or weight."

So one of the boys offered to go after Ne keek.

"What do you think I am?" I objected. "Isn't one fight a day enough?" So we all went out again to play.

We went to school for a half day. The other half was assigned to chore duty. My chore was to go to the garden to pick potatoes or carrots or do whatever needed to be done.

When Bishiu saw me, she said, "I heard about your fight, Way quah. I'm proud of you."

"Well, I wasn't going to let them call me a coward and run over me too much, if I could help it," I told her. But I blushed at her praise.

A few days after this we had a track meet for the small boys. Ne keek was in my group of four or five boys. He came in second.

"You might beat me running, but you haven't beaten me in a fight yet," he boasted. So this left it open for a fight.

When we went into the showers he slapped me on the back. I whirled around to face him and hit back. The other boys were ready with the chips, and again a fight was on. This time we were in our trunks. I discovered that I was really in for a fight. We hurt each other about the face and both of us had black eyes. The older boys had to part us. We hadn't knocked each other down, so I guess we were pretty well matched. But the boys said that I won. They said that I could be a bully now if I wanted to. But I wouldn't pick a fight, although I was ready to give battle if need be. I always tried to settle an argument without a scrap if I could.

Bishiu heard of this as she had of the first scrap. Again she praised me and wrote home to Mother and Min di and told them I was holding my own and that I was doing well in school, too.

Joe Bush and I were still real friends. He was in the same grade as I, and we had much to do together. There were many games of baseball and football, up to Thanksgiving time. After that, the skating started. Near the school was a beautiful lake called White Earth Lake, where we went skating. We made sleds, too, for sliding down a long hill onto the smooth ice of the lake.

Saturday was the time we had to take the girls out on the sleds. Bishiu and I thus had many a pleasant hour together skating and sliding.

Because Mother had no team, we didn't get to go home until Christmas time. It was then the school wagon or sleigh with four horses would take us. There were about twenty children who were thus distributed to their different homes. The horses had sleigh bells, which made our ride a joyous one.

At school we had made up gifts for Mother and Min di. We felt very badly about our home being broken up, because the other children kept telling us what their fathers had done for them. But our father was on another reservation and couldn't keep in touch with us. I don't remember ever having seen him, because we were so small when I left for school the first time.

Mother had always done the best she could for us. When we would go to other homes, I often heard how good our father was and how he had a lumber camp. Often I wondered why he didn't come home to us. But Mother never even mentioned his name in our presence. We never found out what the trouble was. Why had their love departed from the wigwam?

This was the first Christmas at home when little brother Ahmeek and Mah ni had not been with us. How I missed them! I wondered whether they were happy in the shadow land of spirit where they had gone. Or, as I was taught in the white man's belief, had they gone to heaven, where they no longer would suffer as they had suffered here on earth?

Min di helped Mother make gifts for us, and we had a good meal of wild goose. This Wa goosh had shot earlier in the Fall and had frozen it so it would keep.

When finally our Christmas week was over, the school sleigh came after us and once more we had to say goodbye to our home folks. I was fifteen years old now.

With our return to the classroom, schooling went on as before. I was learning much that never would have been taught to me by continuing the ways of my Indian people. My knowledge was coming from books supplied by the white man, not from Nature, which many of the Chippewas still thought was the best teacher.

But I knew then, as I have since, that no amount of such learning that came to me in these schools would keep me from loving the things of Nature. Always would the call of the wolf to its mate stir within me the desire to go again into the forests. Always would the voice of the wind through pine needles or its rustling of the leaves in the sturdy oak and the towering maple bring to me a message that no book could give. Always would I long for the lakes and rivers and the hills.

But now I must do as the white man said, and I did not rebel. So schooling went on as usual. We had our drilling, and I became accustomed to the bugle calls.

Thus winter passed almost quickly. The children got all the seeds ready for planting. In the root cellars of the school, we cut potatoes and sorted the other seeds. We had to clean out the root cellars ready for the new crop in the Fall. As there was no school all summer, we cleaned them and left them up to air out thoroughly.

After our clothing was all packed to go home again, we just had to wait until we had someone to take us.

Joe's father came for him, and the superintendent asked him if he would take us to our home.

Joe's father was tall and strong. His long, straight black hair hung in braids. His brown eyes seemed to be always laughing, and his teeth were white and straight. While I was observing all this, Joe came running over and said we were to go home with him.

We enjoyed the ride, and our hearts sang to the beat of the horses' hoofs.

As it happened, they were going to have a squaw dance that night, and Joe's father was one of the best dancers in that part of the country. We asked Joe if he knew Wa goosh, who was a very good dancer also.

"My father and Wa goosh are very good friends," Joe said.

Joe's father had a beautiful costume. It was of tan buckskin, beaded in leaves, with blossoms and buds on the arms of the shirt. There were fringes on the sleeves and down the trouser legs. He wore beaded moccasins and a deer headdress. This was made of porcupine bristles and looked much like a deer's tail.

We stayed at Joe's home until Mother came, because it was some little ways from home and she was coming to the dance later in the evening.

Wini sisimon (Joe's father's Indian name) and Wa goosh were appointed for the dance contest at the Indian celebration. This was held every June 14 at White Earth Reservation. Indians attended from the different reservations in Wisconsin, North and South Dakota, and even from Montana. Not only Indians came, but white men too. This lasted about a week. It was all Indian doings—pony races, squaw races, dances, and games. Here Wa goosh and Wini sisimon represented the White Earth Reservation Indians. They won first prize for their excellence in dancing.

After this summer we stayed with Mother and

helped her all we could with the berry picking and the rice. Bishiu and I were now able to go out and set nets which Mother had made, and for this work we borrowed Wa goosh's canoe.

Mother told us that next year when we were away at school she would move into a new home that she would build on Bishiu's allotment of eighty acres, which was closer to town and nearer May cha ni, the medicine man.

This year we had to go to school in Beaulieu. It was much nearer to our home, and so it was possible for Mother to come and visit us throughout the holidays. When she came, she was allowed to stay with us from Christmas to New Year's. Many of the boys who had been going to school at White Earth changed with us to Beaulieu. There were now about seventy-five boys and girls here, where the term before there had only been about twenty-five. Joe came too. This year he and I were considered as two of the bigger boys.

Betow drove up with brother Osh kin, and as soon as we could, Bishiu and I went to him and questioned him.

"How does it come you are here?" I asked.

"Well," he replied, a little shamed-faced, "the authorities came after me. I had to go to school."

We then asked if he liked to stay with Betow, or would he rather be with Mother? He didn't know just what to say, because the folks were good to him —but he did miss Mother. He had heard she was going to have a new house; then, maybe, he would return home.

Joe and I took care of the horses. There were two or three bigger boys than we two, but we were well liked and were good students, so we had nice jobs. We were made head of the details. That was to see that the younger boys performed all their work and chores as they should. Some took care of the livestock, and others had to haul wood to each of the different buildings. When not too busy, Joe and I would take the wood on the sleigh and unload it outside, and then the boys would carry it indoors.

During the first term we had to carry all our water from the river, about one and one-half miles distant. We had a "go-devil" sleigh with three barrels on it. These we boys filled and the team would haul the load to the laundry room or kitchen. This became our job each morning after breakfast.

One day about nine in the morning we took the team after the water, and as it was very cold, the reins slipped from my hands while Joe was filling the barrels. The team became frightened and ran away, spilling the barrels of water. The horses were so cold they didn't want to stand. They raced back to the barn and around it two or three times—until at last a farmer stopped them.

He was terribly mad at us. He shouted and scolded, but we couldn't help it. He made us go back with him, but he drove the team himself. He said he would report us to the disciplinarian. This meant we would have to spend our Saturday afternoon, from one to four, splitting wood for the cook stove. This was invariably the punishment for anyone who broke some rule.

I was getting along better, however, at school. I had gotten over some of my bashfulness. We had a wonderful baseball team and played the different towns. Not once that Spring were we beaten. The last game was played at our yearly picnic. This was the regular school picnic, and we always looked forward to it.

During vacation time that year, they dug a well and built a tank about one hundred feet high. On top of this they constructed a windmill. The displinarian asked me if I would climb the windmill and be the "oiler." This had to be done twice a week.

I thought I could do it. He promised me the job when the windmill was finished. It meant that I would have more time for schooling and less work to do.

So at last the time came, when Mother came after us with Way cha, to return home.

CHAPTER IX

INSTEAD of going to our new home, which wasn't finished as yet, we had to return to the shack which was about two miles from Big Ben, and about a mile from Rice River. Osh kin came home with us. We were all terribly disappointed that our new home was not finished.

Early the following morning after our arrival Osh kin and I went for a swim. After getting out of the water, I climbed a tree that was overhanging the river. While lying on a limb I saw a big turtle. I called to Osh kin and said it was down there near him.

He scrambled out and climbed up near to me to see the turtle. It was very large. Osh kin wanted to capture it. He said he would try if I would watch and see that it didn't swim away in the meantime, while he was getting back into the water.

There was about four feet of water here. He knew which way the turtle was headed and could creep up from behind. This he did and grabbed it by one hind leg and the shell. The turtle was nearly as big as a washtub and quite heavy.

But after a moment, Osh kin pulled it up on the bank, and it landed on its back. The Indians believed if a turtle, when thrown like that, landed on its back there would be rain soon.

And sure enough, before we got home this very day it really did rain! It poured down. We were wetter than at the time we were in swimming. Meanwhile, we had used two sticks to make the turtle put out its head. This we grabbed and turned back over the shell. We had no knife, so we had to use a sharp stone to break the turtle's neck.

Now we could carry it between us. How Mother's face lighted up—like the sun on a cloud—when we brought the turtle in. She was proud of us for bringing home such a treat that would make more than one delicious meal.

We asked Mother how long we were going to stay home.

"Only until the new home is finished," she replied. "This will be during the next moon."

We went to work and put in a garden anyway, for later we could return when the crop had matured and harvest it. So we got as busy as beavers and planted about an acre of corn and potatoes.

One day, after we had returned from a swim, Mother asked, "How was the river where you were swimming?"

"Why do you ask?" I wanted to know.

"I thought you could gather some rocks to make a wall across the river," she explained. "It is for a trap to catch fish."

We told her at the swimming hole the water was deep, but that downstream a little ways it was rocky and shallow. She then showed us how to place the rocks across the river to make a wall, almost like a closed V. This we must build up to a height of ten or fifteen inches, forming a sort of trap that would bring the fish down to the center opening, where they could not easily escape until we caught them.

The next morning we arose with the sun and were down by the river while the dew was still wet on the grass and shrubs. It was our plan to make a day of it, so we took our lunch along. Mother, who came a little later, after we had gathered many rocks for the project, now showed us how to make the trap.

One large log was laid across the opening of the V. Then several little poles, about the thickness of a man's wrist and some six feet long, were placed underneath this, about an inch apart. Now when the fish came through this contraption they would flounder around and land on the dry poles. We could always be nearby, so when there were any fish we could gather them up and clean them right on the spot.

This kind of trap only caught the larger fish. At times, when they were not running very fast, we would go upstream and herd them down.

So ended this first day of our fishing by this method that Mother had taught us.

For dinner the next day we had fish, cooked by Mother in the Indian fashion—in smouldering coals.

Later, when we had no use for the trap, it was removed from the river. The fish must not be caught except for eating, for such is the belief of the Chippewas and other Indian tribes.

One day soon after we had cleared away the fish-traps, Betow came to us. He said there were several families going berry-picking. He asked if we would like to go, explaining that he would take his big wagon with his sorrel team.

Of course, we wanted to go! But it was a long trip. For twenty-five miles the wagon rattled along the trail, through forest and over hills, around bogs and across streams. The gentle breeze of the summer day fanned our happy faces and the warm sun smiled down upon us as we jogged on and on. Finally we arrived at our destination, where we were to stay for two weeks, picking the luscious berries. The picking was very good here, so that besides the supply for our own use and for canning we sold many a bushel.

While in town we got the mail. There was a package for me, and there were letters for Mother, which Min di had to read for her. The message was from Cass Lake, from a well-to-do white man up there. He knew both my father and my mother, and said that he wanted to adopt me!

He and his wife had sent many gifts of clothing, and this package to me was one of such gifts that always precede an adoption. In the letter they told how they would send me to college and give me all the advantages of the white boys.

Mother turned to me and asked, "Do you want to go, Son?"

"No," I replied. "Am I not happy in this simple life of the forest and among the many lakes?"

But all through school they continued to send me gifts. But I stubbornly refused to be adopted and remained with Mother. I knew her heart would have been sad had I left the shelter of her love and care to go to the home of a stranger.

The time came when we moved into our new home. How different it was from the one-room wigwam to which we had been accustomed! Despite the fact that this new place was such a departure from the ways of the native Indian life, we all took great pride in fixing it up.

It was a log cabin and gave out a smell of pine and birch. Tall trees towered around the house and there were the merry chirps of birds and the call of wild life, just as it had been before. All that we had given up really was our wigwam with its crude beds and the firepit in the center of the one room.

Now we had three rooms—two of them bedrooms and another that was very large and which was used as a combined kitchen and living room. The roof was thatched, and this, together with the log structure, blended into the surrounding forest so naturally that even an Indian would hardly have found his way to the little clearing without knowing its exact location beforehand.

Our nearest neighbor was half a day's walk through heavy growth of trees and brush, and the only trail was that of the wolf, the deer, or the bear.

All too soon, however, it was school time again. The leaves of the trees were turning brown, and the branches were beginning to show bare, shedding their brown-, red-, and yellow-tinted barbs onto the cool floor of the shadowed forest, covering and protecting the wild flowers that would not again poke their bright faces up through the carpet of leaf mold until after the great snows of the coming winter had melted and O-pee-chee, the robin, returned to sing his happy song.

I had learned to love the primitive life which had for so many, many generations influenced and shaped the existence of my ancestors. But now I must return to the life that the white man had chosen for the Indian to follow—from this time on! I must read from books instead of from Nature. I must learn of the birds and the animals and the trees from books instead of from daily contact with them. This was what the white man said I should do, and I could do nothing but obey.

Again would I forget the language of my people and speak in the tongue of the school. We must all go by the names that had been given us, such as May and John and Caroline and Jim. But among ourselves, however, we would still call each other by our Indian names.

Despite my reluctance to leave the new forest home of my Mother, I could not forget about the windmill. And how proud I was of my new job— my first at the school.

On my first climb up the platform, the disciplinarian went with me. As I ascended each crossbar of the derrick, without one thought of fear, he would ask, "Are you afraid?"

"Afraid!" I laughed. "Of what is there to be afraid?"

But just the same, I was clinging on the rungs of the ladder and climbing upwards with due caution. Never before had I been so high above the ground. And when at last I crawled through the floor of the platform that was around the tank, I stopped for breath and we sat there for a minute just looking. Then we circled around the tank looking over the broad fields and clumps of trees, with the school buildings close by.

As I stood there breathing hard from my climb upwards, I noticed how some trees were taller than others. And then I knew for the first time how the forest and fields and lakes looked to the bird that sailed so freely and happily about. I saw trees that were fat and ancient-looking, others that stood straight and slender, swaying in the wind, and still others that were sturdy and strong, which I knew to be the spreading oak.

I could see the small lake off a little ways among the trees. In the sun's reflection it seemed to smile back at me, and I could see here and there along the shoreline a canoe that had been pulled up from the water and made fast to a sapling or a tree.

Not far away were some cattle nibbling at the brown pasture land. It would be someone's job to milk them nights and mornings.

Looking down again on the school grounds, the children appeared like dolls as they walked along the paths or ran about at play. As I observed all these things, I did not, for a moment, regret my leaving the forest home. Perhaps there were advantages that would make up for what I had left behind!

But now I must climb still higher, up another ladder fastened to the water tank, over the top, then another ten feet to the wheel of the windmill itself. Here I must use even more caution, for a sudden gust of wind might turn the wheel about and sweep me off to the ground below.

The mill had been turned off, so there was little danger in the gentle wind that was blowing. I was shown how to do the greasing, and then, after another lingering look over field and forest, I followed my instructor down. But thereafter I would look forward to this trip and knew that I would each time see something new and interesting.

I was soon to have another job. This was a matter of drilling the boys at school. I learned there was a good baseball team too. I entered into this sport which would give me the exercise I needed to make up for what I would lose without the freedom of life among my own people.

While the cold north wind had not yet come with all its icy breath, we played the game of football. In one such game I was severely hurt; that is, my shoulder was injured. For three weeks I lay in bed and was taken with a sickness that did not come altogether from my shoulder. For a time it seemed that my shoulder and lungs were paralyzed and I found it hard to breathe.

The school doctor who had come to me there on my sick bed returned once more on a day when I was suffering great pain. Surely, he said I would die. It was only a matter of days. But I was not ready to go to the long sleep from which I well knew I would never return. So I prayed to the Great Spirit, which I felt would understand better than would the God of the white man. I prayed that he should come to my bedside and deliver me from the death spirit which hovered very close now, to take me to the shadowland over which he ruled. Thus it was that I remembered the teachings of my Indian people and drew away from what the white man had said I should learn to understand.

The matron there at the school was always very

good and kind to me. When she came into my room she would bring the smile of the sun on her happy, kindly face.

"Have you not a girl friend whom you would like to have sit by your bedside?" she once asked.

I shook my head. I was too bashful to bother with girls.

My sister Bishiu and her friend Lillian came in to see me on a night when I was barely conscious of what went on about me. To the matron's question again, would I not like one of the girls to remain, I answered:

"It is Bishiu that I want. Let her stay."

And so Bishiu did remain at my bedside that night. She must have lain down on the cot next to mine and fallen asleep. Anyway, I didn't see her sitting there beside me when suddenly I heard in the night's stillness the sound of a team outside. When I decided it was a sleigh being dragged across a board walk, the sound ceased. Someone was coming in through the big door in front of the building. Shortly I heard a voice that I knew was my Mother's asking:

"Where can we find Way quah gishig?"

I was fully awake now and tried to call as loudly as I could in my weakened condition, "Here I am, Mother."

In a moment my door was opened and there stood Mother and Min di. It was then that Bishiu jumped up from the cot where she lay. The sleep spirit had not completely left her so that she did not yet know just what was going on. When at last she realized that Mother and Min di had come, she was very happy. My prayer to the Great Spirit had brought the help that I wanted, from my own people!

The three of them came now to my bedside. Not much was said, but Mother and Min di seemed to have a plan. They moved the bed to the middle of the room. Then, seeing that I was snugly tucked in, they just picked up the mattress with me on it and carried me down to the waiting sleigh. On the floor of the sleigh was a lot of nice clean straw on which they placed the mattress. Over me they put a soft feather tick.

All of this time hardly a word was spoken, and I did not question what they intended to do with me. It was enough that Mother and Min di were there, and I was comforted to know that now I would receive the care I needed. The sleigh started off, and after that I remember nothing until later when I lay on my mattress in the home of Wah cha ni, the medicine man, and looked up into their faces.

"Would you like to get up now?" Mother asked.

I tried to rise and with their help I got into a chair. It was Min di who explained that this was my doctor now. He had said I should sit there in a chair by the wood stove and sweat. All this time they were pouring medicine down me. If I wanted to get well, Min di explained, I must do as the medicine man said.

I watched as they made a small wigwam in the big room, and in the center of this they placed some big rocks which were heated. I was told to crawl in and curl around these rocks, but was warned not to touch them. On these hot rocks were certain kinds of herbs that made fumes. This soon gave relief to my tortured lungs. For some time I lay there and the sweat began to form on my body. When finally I was put back to bed I was so weak they had to carry me to the mattress.

It was just a little while after that when Weeng, the sleep spirit, sang to me his lullaby and I slept.

For three days I lay there in the home of the medicine man. And for three days and nights they continued the treatments. Then I knew that Pan Guk, who had beckoned me to the sky trail that led to death, had departed from my sick bed there in the house of the medicine man and that he would not return again to take me.

There were always some folks gathered in the far side of the room and they were telling stories. The one that was sitting watching me saw me smile and soon I was laughing. Then it was they knew for sure that the evil spirits had finally departed.

"Now," said the medicine man, "your Mother and Sister may take you home. But you must remain in bed and keep on taking the medicine, so that you will not again walk so near to the shadowland of death."

I was loaded back on the sleigh and we went on for a few miles in the depth of the forest to Mother's home. Someone went out into the snow-white forest and brought back a rabbit. From this, Mother made some rabbit soup. It was just a week after this that I was outdoors playing. But I was not permitted to go again to school until the great snows had melted, all except for a few patches under the trees in the surrounding forest. And there were signs that the Spring would soon return to bring new life to the barren earth.

CHAPTER X

I WAS welcomed with open arms by the children and teachers alike. By their smiles and the many kindnesses they showered upon me, I was made to feel that their hearts were warm and that I would have been missed had I never returned. I soon caught up to the others in my studies.

There came a day not long after Gee wah de hohn, the North wind, had gone back to his home in the far northland when the bright, warm face of the sun had melted even the patches of snow in the deepest shadows of the forest. All roads and trails were still very muddy under the heat of the sun, though at night there would sometimes be a slight freeze. We were all at the table for our noonday meal when a spirited team of horses drove up to the school gates, and the disciplinarian went out to see who it could be. In a minute he returned.

"Bishiu," he called. "It is for you. Please come."

My sister left the table, and soon thereafter we were all dismissed to go about as we pleased until time for classes. While brother and I tarried outside, wondering to whom Bishiu was talking, the disciplinarian called to us:

"Don't you boys know this man who is talking to your sister?"

We shook our heads. He was a total stranger to us. Never had we seen him. Then he said:

"He is your own father. You may go to him if you wish."

So after all these years I was to meet my father . . . the father about whom I had so often wondered . . . the mate of my mother! In their hearts the love song no longer was heard, and so he had departed from the wigwam where we children were born.

At seeing us once again, my father's joy was great. We talked long in the language of the Chippewas, and many things did he relate as to what had happened during the years of our separation.

But we were told that not a word should be spoken about this meeting to Mother. We promised. Then he gave each of us a dollar. He was a tall and very straight and handsome man, with piercing dark eyes and fine features.

He wrote on a piece of paper the place where he lived. I knew then it was near the home of the people who for so long had wanted to adopt me. These people were the ones who had said they knew my father. It was up North at Cass Lake. I knew then that some day, after I grew older, I would make a journey up there. But I would never allow myself to be adopted by these people who wanted me.

It was now the time of the year that the loggers started the river drive. The gates of the dam would be opened, which would let out the water and fish. The water at this time was always very muddy, for the men sluiced the logs through the dam and on down the river. This operation would scare the fish, so they would go up the little streams and creeks that empty into Rice River.

On a Saturday afternoon most of the larger boys were allowed to go fishing. As the afternoon sun began to drop below the tops of the nearest trees, we had already caught enough fish to supply the whole school for our coming Sunday dinner.

The warm days of the early summer were now upon us. The robin found its mate and the mother bird was setting on her eggs, while the father bird brought worms and other choice things for her to eat. Always would he sit protectingly near while the little ones pecked their way through the shells under the feathered body of the mother. Squirrels scampered merrily about on the twig-covered ground, or chattered from branches of oak or fir and spruce.

My heart sang with joy as the end of the school drew near. For I longed for the freedom that life at home would again bring to me. I wanted to roam the forest trails that I had learned so well—to track the deer, to listen to the call of wild things, and to breathe the sweet incense of forest shrubs and trees and herbs. Lake and river and stream called to me as they could only call to one who understands the ways of the Indian. There was the canoe in which I would glide swiftly over the rippling waters where

I would see in the mirror-like depths the reflection of tall pines and spreading oaks.

Who, I wondered, would come after us this time? Who would come with team and wagon to take us over the forest trails to the log cabin where now our Mother waited for us? Not only would we revert again to the Indian life, but we would once more take on our Indian names of Way quah and Bishiu, and Osh kin. And it would still be Min di for my oldest sister at home. Mah ni and little brother Ahmeek had already gone to their new home over the long sky trail from which they would never return, the same journey on which Pan Guk had not many moons ago beckoned me, but over which I had refused to go.

It so happened that Betow came first after Osh kin. Bishiu and I went home with them. We stopped at Uncle Snow Cloud's for a visit, and Osh kin also remained there with us for the time.

I learned now that our sister Min di had married. But her love had not been for the one I had thought —Wa goosh. It was for a John Chompson (Chaney), a half-blood who had sung his love song during the winter that had just passed. She had known this was the man who would make her heart sing with happiness. Chaney was a big-boned, sandy-haired fellow. He was tall and strong, and his smile was pleasant and friendly to all whom he met. He was a lumber-jack and liked working in the great woods. He immediately made up with us children, and we liked him from the beginning.

Betow, who had a good team, offered to plow up

some of our land for a garden. It was he and Chaney who prepared the two acres and put in the crop. We all helped, for we wanted this done before Uncle Snow Cloud came to take us with him on a trip to Leach Lake.

He and his wife had been to visit her folks at Nahnomen. They remained with Mother a few days, and then we packed our clothes to go with him. Betow drove us down to the train at Lengby. We journeyed to Walker and from there packed our things to the shores of Leach Lake. Here Uncle had his big canoe, and we paddled across the Lake to a friend's home in Oengum.

This man was a bachelor. He was very nice to us. Uncle made arrangements with him to take us by wagon to Little Boy Lake, where he would meet us, as he was going back to Walker for provisions. Then he would come across Leach Lake into Boy River and down to another river, then to Little Boy Lake.

We climbed into the wagon to which was hitched his team of little Indian ponies. This was a very nice trip. Over hills and prairies we drove. Through the beautiful forests of maple, birch, oak, cedars, and tall pines. There were many more different kinds, too, and different hues. When finally we came out of the forest, we were on the high banks of Little Boy Lake. This too was beautiful, to stand there on the high bluffs and see so many miles around with the sun smiling at us from the smooth water and the trees showing upside down along the shore line.

We made camp here for a couple of days till

Uncle could make the trip back from Walker with the provisions for us all. He would have quite a load. We camped up on one of these bluffs so we could watch down the river.

In a few days there came five canoes up the river. Instead of coming towards us, however, we were surprised to see them turn to the left, and we could see them unloading all their food and things on the shore. One of the canoes after unloading, came over towards us and it was then we knew it was really Uncle. He came across Little Boy Lake to us and said he wanted to camp over there. So we soon had all our things over there with them. This friend of Mother's and his had unhitched his team and let them loose, because he was going along with us.

When we got to Uncle's camp, we found the five families who had come along with Uncle. Aunt Isabelle and Uncle Tom were there. Uncle had met them and invited them all along.

We remained for three days while Uncle and his wife went to his cabin home to get another row-boat. There were too many of us for the canoes.

Mother and Min di paddled them across the river and they walked from there. It was half a day's walk through the forest to their log cabin. They came back up the river and Uncle turned the boat over to Mother, explaining that we must be careful with it, as it was a very good one.

After noon lunch, Uncle Tom went out hunting. He made his way through the swamp into a very dark, dense, hardwood forest, and was gone for about an hour. Then we heard a shot. Half an hour later he returned and on his face was a big smile. He asked Aunt Isabelle if she would like to come with him.

He had shot a bear, and it had fallen into the crotch of a tree. He would have to chop the tree down. That was why he came back—for an axe.

My aunt asked Mother if Osh kin and I could come along. We were very excited, because he thought there would be several cubs around there.

We took our hatchets, intending to be of help. As we went through the dark swamps and came to a heavy hardwood forest, Osh kin kept showing me what he would do if a bear came between us. He took his hatchet and hit hard on a tree as he exclaimed, "This is the way I'll hit him—right on the head!"

Shortly we came to a little rise in the forest and Uncle said:

"Look over there closely and you can make out the bear in that tree. We must be watchful as there might be another bear around—the dead one's mate."

As we came to a windfall, Uncle climbed over it and turned to tell Aunt to go around, for it was very large. He said to go around towards the roots, which were turned up. While she was walking around the roots she called to Uncle to knock on the windfall because she was sure it was hollow. She had seen something dark inside.

I had climbed up on top and Osh kin was still on the ground. Uncle pounded on the windfall, and sure enough, two little cubs came right out where Aunt stood. She chased them and they came right back between Osh kin and me. When Osh kin saw them he turned and ran so fast that we didn't have time to stop him. The funny part of it was that he had made no trail to follow back—but he never stopped until he reached camp.

Uncle chopped the tree down, and after it had fallen the bear didn't move. But Uncle was very careful—so he hit it again on the head to make sure the bear wasn't just stunned.

Uncle and Aunt skinned him and cut him up so we could each carry some. Pack straps were made of wegoob.

We got back to camp in time to have the liver and heart for supper. The rest was cut up, and most of it was prepared to dry. We divided the meat among the six families.

Since the rice was not quite ready to harvest, the folks decided to stay right there a few more days and get the bear meat dried so it could be packed away and handled easily.

When they thought the rice was ready to harvest, we started down the river into a lake. From there we moved on into another river and then into another lake. Here we pulled up on dry land and unloaded.

Now we had to portage about one-fourth of a mile to Thunder Lake. The women and children carried all the lighter stuff, while the men carried the boat. It was so heavy it took four men, so as not to make it too heavy for any one man. Then they came back for the canoes. These one man could handle, but to make it easier, two men got under each one. They turned them upside down and put their heads inside and carried them this way. We children had made several trips, and shortly all the supplies were over on Thunder Lake.

We then went down the river into Rice Lake. This was where Uncle's log cabin was. We had a nice trip and were soon settled at Uncle's home, where we made ready for the gathering of the rice.

The rice harvesting lasted about three weeks. Each family had about six hundred pounds to take home with them.

We returned the same way we had come up. When we got on Leach Lake this time, it was very rough, so we all stopped at the house of a friend of Mother's. Min di, Mother, and Bishiu went to the house first. Mother opened the door and sister and Bishiu stepped in. Just as she did, a partridge flew into the window and broke it. Everyone scrambled for the bird, and they looked at Bishiu. For it is an old Indian belief that the person who entered first under such circumstances would not live long. Nothing, however, was said about this for her ears to hear. But all the older ones knew this was a bad sign and something was going to happen.

The next morning the lake was smooth again. We continued on our way. We stopped at Bear Island and had dinner and then went on to Walker. Here we got a train for Lengby, where Betow met us and took us home.

CHAPTER XI

THAT FALL I got my first job. Ten dollars a month and room and board! It was on a farm, and I worked for this man all through the winter and on into the summer.

That fall, Mother was going back to Uncle Snow Cloud's to make rice. They were going to gather some rice to sell, for they had been blessed with a good crop.

At Christmas time, when I finally returned home, I noticed that Bishiu was absent.

"Where is Sister?" I demanded, knowing even before the answer came that something was wrong. Mother sat there in silence not looking at me. The lines in her face seemed deeper and she looked much older.

After a while Min di came over to me and said:

"Way quah, do you remember the partridge— the one that flew through the window glass and broke it there in front of Bishiu?"

I nodded and just stood staring at her. It was plainly written in her face that some sort of tragedy had come to Bishiu.

"Tell me," I said at last. "What is it that has happened to Sister?"

"Our Sister's face will never smile at us again," said Min di. "Her feet will no longer go over the forest trail. Her voice will not be heard at play. Pan Guk came while you were gone and took her from us."

"But what made her die?" The words choked in

my throat. I had loved Bishiu very deeply. We had been inseparable all these years.

"We do not know," said Min di gently. "We were on the lake and had camped at Pelican Island. Suddenly she took sick. It might have been a poison herb that she ate by mistake. Before we could get her to a medicine man she had gone from us."

"Where . . . where did you . . . put . . . her?" I faltered. I could not keep back the sob in my voice.

"We just buried her there on the island. The lake was so rough we could not bring her home. It was so far away from any town and there was no way to get lumber for her coffin."

"Did . . . did you mark the grave?" I asked, resolved that I would go there at the first opportunity.

"Oh yes, Way quah. Your Uncle Snow Cloud was with us and he knew the way they buried their dead long before wooden coffins were brought to us by the white man. We made a frame of white cedar, something like the shape of a small canoe. This we covered with birch bark. The bed was of fine cedar boughs, and covering all was birch bark. Placing the body in this, we sealed the whole thing with pitch, which made it air and water proof."

"It is good." I said after a moment. "Bishiu would have had it no other way—for she had told me so more than once. She wanted to be buried the Indian way."

It was a very sad Christmas for me. They told me that Uncle had lost his wife, too, only last week. He was coming to stay the rest of the winter with us.

If I wished, I could return with him when he left for home in the spring.

When finally he arrived, he and I had many good times on the forest trails, hunting, trapping and fishing on the lake.

Then it came the time when the heavy snow of the winter began to melt under the bright, warm sun of the early spring. Soon now Uncle would leave us and I was sad over the prospect. He had done much to help me forget my loss of Bishiu.

Then one day when the robin again sang cheerily in the tree near our home and the bare earth was beginning to take in some of the warmth of the sun, Uncle came up to me where I sat under a great oak tree and said:

"I've been thinking that it would be well if you could return to my home with me. There would be fewer mouths for your mother to feed. My home will be very lonely now that my wife has gone never to return. And there is much I can teach you . . . much that you will need to know after you are a man. Will you go?"

I jumped up all excited. "Oh, Uncle Snow Cloud," I cried, "could it be you understood why it was I was so sad? Could you know it was because of your leaving?"

He took me by the shoulders and looked me squarely in the eyes. "I thought as much. Come— we shall tell your Mother."

Mother, of course, was sad when we told her. But I knew she had been expecting it. "You will return to me soon?" she asked.

"Yes, Mother," I replied.

Mother then became very busy preparing for my departure—getting ready the clothes I would need.

Soon we were ready to start. On the day we said our farewell to home and those who remained, Uncle said:

"Let us stop by and ask John Cloud if he wants to make this trip with us."

This we did, and when we got there, we discovered that Mack quah was visiting him. They both would go with us.

We remained with them overnight to give their wives time to assemble the equipment and food that would be needed on this trip, which my Uncle thought might require three or four weeks.

All this time I had not forgotten my resolve to go to the grave of Bishiu. So now I reminded Uncle that we could stop at the little island where she was buried. To this he agreed.

When the middle of the first day came we pulled our canoes up onto the shore of Pelican Island. The sun had gone down behind a dark cloud and the wind blew quite hard. It seemed that rain was not far off.

Immediately as I put foot on the island, a strange spell came over me. The trees seemed to bow their heads before the wind in reverence to the one who lay in the Indian grave somewhere under their swaying branches.

In just a little while Uncle Snow Cloud had led me to Bishiu. "This is the place," he told me.

"When you are ready to leave, we will be waiting for you by the canoes at the lake shore."

When he had gone, I stood there silently, watching. Bishiu had said if she went to the land of Souls before I did, she would always be at my side to advise and guide me whenever I needed her. And I needed her now if ever I would! A great loneliness had come over me for this one who had played with me and joined me on the forest trails. Would she come to me now, as she had said she would?

The wind moaned through the trees and I listened for any message they might bring. For it is the Indian belief that the Great Spirit speaks through nature; that the earth breathes messages that he should hear; that the lakes and rivers talk to him and give helpful counsel; that there are happenings which may occur while he is sitting quietly before his fire in the wigwam or on the hunt over forest trail—warnings, perhaps, to which he should give careful heed.

As I stood there, I became suddenly conscious that a new brightness had come over the earth. I looked up, and the sun was smiling at me through a wide rift in the clouds. The wind had gone down and a gentle, warming breeze touched my cheek.

At that moment all the gloom that had pressed down on my heart began to drift away. It was as though Bishiu had indeed spoken, that her spirit had returned from the land of Souls to comfort the one who had been left behind to sorrow. I left this spot that would always remain sacred and returned to the lake shore, knowing then without a doubt that Bishiu would indeed always be by my side until I joined her in the spirit world.

So it was with a lighter heart that I rejoined my uncle at the place by the lake shore where they had waited for me.

The storm that had threatened when first we pulled the canoes up on the shore had now passed by. Dark clouds still hovered low over the western horizon, but the sun shone brightly overhead and there was just enough wind to stir the lake into little ripples. Soon we had pushed off for the shore that lay towards the rising sun.

Before nightfall, we had carried our canoes to another, smaller lake and paddled across to the opposite shore where we made camp. Starting early next morning we progressed by a series of lakes and streams until finally we reached my uncle's home, which was on the northern shore of Rice Lake.

The first thing we did here was to go into the swamp and gather cedar boughs with which to cover the canoes. Meanwhile, however, we had turned them upside down to keep the sun from melting the pitch in the seams. Uncle said to me:

"Way quah, go unlock the house and see whether or not it has been disturbed. The bears here are very bothersome at times, and the house will need airing, too, before we can stay there."

I found everything in order and was soon back at the lake to help the men carry the food stuff and other supplies to the cabin. John Cloud and Mack quah asked me if I wanted to go with them or remain and help Uncle. For they were going to gather enough wood to last the visit. I said:

"Oh, I will stay right here with Uncle. I want to help him around the cabin."

There was much to do before we went on for the hunting we had planned. This hunt was to be like a vacation. We would go down the river to Brainard by canoe, trapping, hunting and fishing all the way.

Next we proceeded to nail boards over the windows, for the bears were very inquisitive. They liked to climb up to a window, and if they saw anything inside that looked appetizing, they would just break in and help themselves.

I did all that I could to assist Uncle with the evening meal—like hauling the water and making a place out on the ground where we could spread the food. I also carried some of the wood indoors, so we would be sure to have enough dry wood when later we returned from our trip.

John Cloud and Mack quah had much to do also, such as cleaning their guns and making stretchers for muskrat, mink, wolves, and any other animals we might catch.

We gathered many long sticks for staking the traps into the water wherever we found a muskrat mound. These traps all had to be worked over so they would trip easily. Uncle had about seventy-five of these steel traps, which were so fitted up that they would spring with a very light touch. We would use some kind of animal fat to oil the hinges, for with wild animal fat the human scent is killed better than would be possible with any other oil.

Of course, this was all strange to me, and I was anxious to try my skill. So I said to Uncle, "I wish you would let me set a trap or two."

"Tomorrow," he replied with a smile, "you shall have your wish."

And so on the next day he showed me how to set traps for the muskrat, the mink, and the coon. The mink and coon traps were to be set very much alike, so when you expect a mink you may find a coon instead.

For me this was a very exciting period of my life. To have these braves and my Uncle give me so much attention, to teach me so many things that would make of me the great hunter I wanted to be, was an honor indeed. And they, seeing that I was such an apt pupil, showed pleasure in all they did to help me. Their faces would light up at the way I responded to it all. I was encouraged to be very alert to their every suggestion.

This evening, while the sun yet showed its fiery face just before it left the earth in darkness and started on its night sky trail, I worked hard and fast until the food was ready on the table. We all ate heartily and soon afterward went to bed. But the sleep spirit did not come to me at once, nor to the others. For they told stories of the Indian legends. And so I lay there for a long time, just listening. Once in a while one of them would say, "Are you still awake, Way quah?"

And I would answer, "Yes," and then they would continue.

Finally, though, sleep took me and they went right on till the story being told was finished. When next morning I awoke, I asked them about the ending of the legend, and said I wanted to hear it all.

"Never mind," I was told. "When we are going on downstream, you shall hear what happened from the time you fell asleep."

With the morning meal, a new storyteller was appointed for that night. This time it would be Mack quah. I resolved that I would prepare so that Weeng wouldn't sing to me his sleep lullaby this night until I was ready for him. But I needn't worry, said my Uncle. Should sleep claim me before the story's ending, I could hear the rest of it on the next day in the canoe. I could change to the boat of Mack quah. They were all so good to me. I felt proud to claim them as friends.

Breakfast over, John Cloud and Mack quah went to cut their poles. Uncle advised me to stay close to the house because he was going to take me out for a canoe ride. He wanted to see whether we could get some wild duck for dinner. So while he got his guns ready, I stayed very close to the cabin. Then we both started for the canoe.

Suddenly I heard a noise behind me. I turned and there was a white horse coming our way, and a man was on its back. This was not an Indian pony that he rode.

As Uncle turned to look, too, the horse and rider

came up swiftly and a man stepped from the saddle. He raised his hand in salute, Indian fashion, but I could see at once that he was not an Indian.

"Booshu," he greeted my Uncle. This meant, "Hello."

And then for some reason I became frightened. Perhaps it was because of a guilty conscience that I was not in school where I belonged. Maybe this white man had come to take me back! Then I would miss this wonderful hunting trip which meant much more to me than all the schooling they could possibly give me.

I was beginning to realize that I was being forced to give up all that was dear to me, and it was not good that this should be done. Nothing the white man could teach me would take the place of what I was learning from the forest, the lakes, and the river. I could read more in the swaying of the trees and the way they spread their branches and leaned to the wind than I could read in any books that they had at school. I could learn much more from the smiling, rippling waters and from the moss and the flowers than from anything the teachers could tell me about such matters. I could study the ways of the birds, the wild things of field and forest. I could gain knowledge from my daily walks under the trees where the shadows mixed with the shifting sunlight and the wind fanned my cheek with its gentle caress or made me bend, as it did the trees, to its mighty blasts.

I spoke to the man in English.

"What do you want?" I asked.

He seemed surprised that I could talk his language. He knew then I had been away attending some government school.

"What school is it you go to?" he asked. "Did you run away? How long have you gone there?"

All these questions frightened me all the more, but I tried hard not to let him know that I feared him.

"Just what is it you want here?" I asked again.

"Oh, I just came over to see Snow Cloud. You see, we have been very good friends for a long time. I heard someone chopping wood, so I rode over here to see who it was disturbing the place. It might be Snow Cloud, I thought. We have missed him since he went away last Fall. When he leaves, I come past once in a while to see that everything is all right," he explained.

Now that I realized he had not come to take me away, I changed my attitude towards him and he told me how many times he had come over to Uncle's to teach him English. Uncle in turn had taught him Indian. They had also exchanged different foods and various articles—such as tea, sugar, and flour for buckskin gloves or anything else we had. Since this was quite a distance from town, the arrangement had been very convenient.

"And you are Snow Cloud's son?" he inquired.

"No," I replied, "but he sometimes calls me Snow Cloud."

"Then you are going to stay here with him?" he asked.

"I don't know," I answered. "I have come with

him this time just to learn what he can teach me of hunting and trapping and fishing. I want so much to learn all that I can about such things; for this the white man's school cannot teach me."

"You speak very good English," he praised me. "I think it would be a big help to him if he kept you for an interpreter."

"I see you are ready to leave," he said, without waiting for me to reply. He looked around at the guns, packs, and other equipment.

"Yes, my uncle had promised me this trip down the Mississippi River. We are to go hunting, trapping, and fishing. With us will go John Cloud and Mack quah, who are out in the woods cutting poles to hold down the traps."

Soon the two braves returned, and this man, whose name was Henry, invited us all to have dinner with him. We accepted, and now it was I who discovered that Henry could talk quite good Indian.

Later in the afternoon we paddled around the lake shore to set a few traps. I was watching with eyes alert and ears wide open. Nothing that any of them did escaped me. Shortly Uncle had shot several mallard ducks. When finally we had finished setting the traps we returned to the cabin where he dressed the ducks and put them in the place he had prepared for keeping things cold. This was a niche in the side of the wall where the water fell over from the nearby spring. The place was walled with cedar.

Not until the next day would we need the ducks. Snow Cloud and Mack quah had come back by now, and they had a pot of wild wintergreen tea all ready for us. There was fried bread for the meal. This bread was made to fry or bake, whichever way one wanted it. It is a mixture of flour and milk and salt. It is cooked in a pan of fat and fried to a nice brown.

After we had finished this meal, we made preparations to go to Henry's. His house was half a mile distant and we had to walk. There were no trails. But the Indians found the way easily even through the thick pine forest, and I did not object to the way we were forced to break the trail as we went.

Henry's buildings consisted of two big barns and other long buildings. I learned that he was a watchman for a lumber company. This summer, however, there was no logging going on. We were taken around and shown the entire property—his cows, horses, pigs, and chickens. His was just a small farm, and after looking over the place we also went to the camp. After this inspection Henry told me to play outside while he got the evening meal on the table. But I told him that I would much rather help him.

There were many questions I wanted to ask. While he had been showing me around the lumber camp I had been busy thinking. All these beautiful trees that the Indian loved so much were being destroyed. What would happen to our great forests if this kept up? Where would the Indian hunt? What would the animals do who lived there? The braves who had come with us were asking the same questions, and I was troubled. It was the Indian instinct having its way with me again.

My troubled thoughts were broken into by the

call to eat. And what a feast that was! Much like a big Thanksgiving meal. There was steak, mashed potatoes, string beans, and gravy. We finished with peaches for dessert. And the pleasure we got from eating was matched by Henry's joy over having us share his cooking. He said he was thus having the chance to return all that Uncle had done in teaching him about the ways of the forest and the wildlife that made its home there.

He expressed the wish that he could remain always with Uncle. "Perhaps the government will open up some homesteads here, and if they do I'll sure get one."

We talked for an hour after the feast and then we made our way back to the cabin. When returning, we took the short-cut back—the way that was nearest the lake. On this trail we came upon some red willows; or kinnkinic. Uncle always carried his hatchet with him, and we stopped while he cut ten sticks, each three feet long. After the others expressed a desire to have some, too, he cut more for them.

Home at the cabin a fire was built outside and there we sat before the sparkling, crackling fire talking of all that we planned to do on our trip down the river. Meanwhile the men were busy stripping the bark off the willows. This bark was like that of the cherry tree, and it was to be dried on these same poles from which it was taken.

While they sat and smoked, a story was suggested. Mack quah, who that morning had been appointed the storyteller for this evening, said he would tell the story of the Red Willow. He related how Nana bush was a superman of the Chippewas, how he performed great deeds and nothing could harm him.

Nana bush came to his canoe by the lake shore one day. He sat down on a log and scratched his head wondering what he was going to do. "I'm hungry," he thought to himself. "The time has come to eat. We will have a duck dinner."

He looked out over the lake and saw many different kinds of ducks and wondered which would taste the best.

So Nana bush busied himself and started a roaring fire close to the log he was sitting on. Seeing such a good fire, he said, "One of each of the ducks will I call." He called to the ducks to fly around over his head in a circle. He told them to close their eyes and fly low enough so that he might touch them, so he could grab them by the feet. But he also warned them that the one who first opened his eyes before being given permission would then have red eyes.

And as each of the various kinds passed him, he would grab one and wring its neck. Then he covered it with clay, which was already by his side, and finally stuck its head down in the ashes. Pretty soon he had one of each kind except for one; this was the Hell Diver. But just then it opened one eye and saw Nana bush and that he had grabbed one. He perceived what was happening. So quickly he called to the rest of the ducks, "He is killing all of us—let us fly away!"

And so the ducks all disappeared, and there was

no Mr. Hell Diver in Nana bush's collection. From this time on the Hell Diver has had a red eye—the only duck with such a one.

By now the ducks he had buried in the ashes were great in number. They made a complete circle around his large fire. He had to leave to gather more wood. Upon his return he felt weary and said to himself, "I will lie down here nearby and rest myself."

He lay awhile thinking of the good feed he would have when all the fowl were done—but finally he went to sleep. When he awoke, he thought he had slept many hours, but upon looking at the fire and seeing the way it burned, he knew well he had been asleep only a short time. Quickly he got up and walked around the fire testing the ducks. If the feet of the fowl pulled away with no effort, it was done —but should the feet not pull away, then the fowl was not yet done.

Nana bush thought it was not time enough for them to be done, but he tried anyway. Then he went to lie down again. He feared, lest the sleep spirit might keep him too long under its influence and he would not hear if anyone should try to steal the ducks from the fire. But he was so sleepy by this time he had to lie down. As he did so he raised his head and said, "Watching Eye, tell me if anyone comes around."

Soon he was fast asleep. Yet while he slept, his stomach started growling and he thought he heard his "Watching Eye" calling. So he raised up and looked around, but no one could he see. He fell asleep again. It seemed that within a few minutes his "Watching Eye" called again, but he was so tired that he paid no attention. And while he was heavy in sleep two men came and saw him. After taking all the fowl they put the duck's feet back in the ashes again, just like Nana bush had left them. And when Nana awoke the two men had the ducks and were gone.

He raised up and was filled with a great hunger. Rising, he stretched and yawned, and thought, "Now for a good feast."

He started for the first duck. And so easy did its feet pull out that he said, "Ah ta ya may wee sha minu su inge bah," meaning, "Cooked a long time and well done."

He went on to the next and the next—then after trying them all he threw the feet into the fire and picked up a stick so that he could dig for the ducks. But he went all around the fire and, to his bewilderment, he could not find one duck. He looked up at the sun and exclaimed: "I slept not so long that they would burn up. Someone has taken them."

He questioned the "Watching Eye" and all it would do was grunt. Then it said it had tried to waken him, but that Nana bush had turned over and would not wake up. Still Nana bush accused it, so he got a switch and started hitting the "Watching Eye"—which was himself. He didn't think that was enough punishment, so he got another switch off a thorn bush and continued punishing himself. Still he thought this was not enough. He looked at the fire and saw a hot coal. This he went to and sat on,

squirming around with pain. But this was not sufficient. He walked along the lake shore where there
was a clump of underbrush. He sat down in it and
squirmed just like he did in the fire. When he
turned around and looked at the brush, it was all
red with the blood from the punishment he had
given his "Watching Eye." And though it was part
of him, he being the higher man was not harmed.
So this is how the red willow got its name.

When Mack quah had finished telling of this tra-
ditional story of the Chippewa tribes, I was strong
with desire to sleep. It was only a short time when I
was journeying in the land of dreams.

CHAPTER XII

AFTER breakfast the next morning, Uncle Snow
Cloud called to me to go with him to look over
his traps. He wanted me to understand how they
were set and to know where they were, for next time
he would not go with me.

We got the canoe into the water. Uncle put me
in the bow of the canoe. We started to paddle, but
soon he corrected me on the hard work I was making out of it.

"Stop and watch me," he instructed. "It is not
such hard work if you know how."

We nosed into the shore, and he pointed. "Do
you see that trap?"

I could see a stake and as I followed the chain
down to the trap I saw that it was empty. I noticed

how it had been placed in the bog on the muskrat's trail.

Uncle then asked me what I saw, and I told him. He was pleased with the things I noticed. This was one way of setting the trap—but no two were ever set quite alike.

"As I paddle you up to the next one, you can see how it is set and where it is placed," he said.

We discovered that we had caught two muskrats in all. I learned that whenever we got a catch, the trap was never set there again for a few days, as the muskrat will not come near his home for some time if it has been disturbed.

We anchored the canoe in the water because I was going to go on my own in the afternoon.

Uncle Snow Cloud now said he would look things over and get our equipment together for the hunting trip. While he was doing this, John Cloud and Mack quah set out to look over the different kinds of berry bushes to see if there was going to be enough fruit to justify bringing their families down for picking.

This left me alone, so I soon climbed into the canoe and set out with five or six traps. My, was I a great hunter! I had to remember exactly where I put the traps. So, where there wasn't a landmark, I would tie the growing grasses into a knot. If there were willows, I would break a branch and let it hang.

When I got back, Uncle Snow Cloud asked me if I had set all my traps. I smiled and said I had.

I soon became worried about John Cloud and

Mack quah, as they hadn't as yet returned home. Uncle Snow Cloud told me not to worry; they were Indians and so knew the forest trails very well.

When they finally returned they showed some disappointment that there weren't as many berries as they had expected. Not enough to bother with. They would be on the lookout now for another place where berry picking was good.

I was anxious to go to bed, because it was John Cloud's turn to tell a story, but this time I fell asleep before he had finished.

I didn't awaken the next morning until they called me and announced that breakfast was ready. Was I surprised! I had been accustomed to rising with the break of day.

When we were through, Uncle Snow Cloud said, "Well, Way quah, now we'll see how good a trapper you are. You have set your own traps—but I'm going with you to see how well you have done it." He had changed his mind about sending me alone.

Not long did it take him to discover where I had set the traps. It pleased him to see I knew how to do it without destroying the ground or plant life. He couldn't say too much, anyhow, because I caught one muskrat to match the only one he could show for his own effort.

On this trip we gathered all our traps, for we would be on our way early the next morning. We dressed our rats and put their skins on stretchers.

Before the sun's rays had colored the tall tree tops the next morning, we were headed for the river. We paddled along slowly and silently. Nothing hap-

pened to disturb the peace and beauty of our surroundings. We stayed close together so we could
talk back and forth.

At noon we pulled up to the shore and made a
fire. We were ready for our meal, and then we
stretched out, or ran around to rest ourselves. We
remained there on shore for an hour or so and then
pushed off again. The air was so warm and the winds
so gentle we didn't have to make much of a camp at
night. We had just our fire and lay around it. We
slept under the stars.

We still had our stories every night and pushed
out early again each morning. This we did for three
or four days. Then about one-fourth of a mile from
the lake, Mack quah stood up in his canoe and
looked out over the bog towards the lake shore.
Seeing all the muskrat mounds, he said, "It is good
that we stop here. Let us make our camp here for a
while." We were all tired of canoeing so much, and
we could see the lake was stirred by an angry spirit.

We camped here, and Uncle said that while he
was getting supper he wanted me to take the shot-
gun and go into the forest. He thought I might be
able to shoot a partridge or prairie chicken as a
change from the food we had brought along.

But the hunting on this day was not good for me,
and when I returned I was heavy of heart. I had
shot nothing. And I did want to find favor in my
uncle's eyes.

They knew the lake was too rough to set traps,
so John Cloud and Mack quah set about twenty-
five on the river banks leading down to the lake.

Long after sunrise we slept, but upon arising we went to the shore and could see by their faces they had made a good catch. This meant we would have a good meal of boiled muskrat.

With a light heart we prepared the meat and put the skins on stretchers. It was a big task for me, but a very interesting one, and my heart sang with the joy of doing it. Muskrat, I had learned, is very delicious if prepared properly.

Uncle took me out in the woods and showed me the most likely trees in which to find partridges. He pointed some out to me and I shot at them. Some I brought down. He praised me for sureness of eye. But he said I was not nearly as good as my father and that I had much to learn to be able to live up to him. He was always praising my father and often remarked on how much I resembled him.

Uncle Snow Cloud pointed out buds, berries, and mosses that the different kinds of animals and birds ate. By knowing these, one could tell which animal or bird was in that vicinity. He taught me how to make snares for deer, deadfalls for bears and wolves, and trap-cages for owls and eagles. We used the feathers from owls and eagles for headdresses and dance costumes.

All this time the lake kept getting rougher and rougher. So one morning when we awoke and the lake was again peaceful and seemed to reflect the blessing of the great spirit on our continued journey, we decided it was time to move on.

The water was like a great mirror, and the big trees were silhouetted on the surface.

Our canoes made ripples on the water and it made a beautiful sight. Our hearts were glad just to be there.

The two braves broke into song with their beautiful Indian words. My ears were open to all they did and soon I joined in with my little voice. This gave them much pleasure. Ours was a happy carefree life.

On and on we traveled for days, on through the lake and down the Willow River, until we saw a place where we could get in some good trapping.

Now it was my and Uncle's turn to see how many animals we could catch. John Cloud and Mack quah had their turn the last stop.

We bragged that "we would show them up." We had quite a time—all in fun. After landing and unloading, Uncle and I were soon out with our traps. It was their turn to make camp while we were out. On that first day we didn't do so well. But we had to brag about our exploits. So I said, "Just wait till I learn more about animals and their ways—I'll show you I can be a great hunter such as you are now. Soon I will learn to set my own traps." All of the time I was trying to plan how I could get off by myself.

Another day came, and the others were all busy with something else, so I sneaked off. They probably knew I was up to something—but they were too wise to interfere. They just let me go. That night I couldn't sleep on account of the excitement of imagining what might be waiting for me on the morrow. There were more stories, and I heard them through. Noticing this, they wanted to know what the trouble was. Was it because I was beginning to long for my mother's cabin or for my brothers and sisters? Had I decided that hunting for me was much better closer to home where the trails were well broken and the voices of the wild creatures were more familiar to my ears?

I did not deny that their words were true. But the next morning I went about my own plans, and that did not include them. I went off by myself and guarded carefully what I had in mind to do. I should have known, though, that I couldn't keep such things from an Indian. They have a way of noticing all the little movements of the nerves, and this would speak to them more loudly than would my words.

Later, they had returned with their catch of muskrat, mink, and coon and were very happy over their success. Soon they were busy fixing the skins.

I decided now was the time. Never did I suspect they were watching me all this time. Anyhow, they let me go without a word.

Now I was in the canoe and paddled quite a distance down the river to where I had set my traps. From there I worked my way back toward camp. Long before it was time for the sun to go down behind the trees in the west I was back. To my surprise I saw my uncle and the others at the shore awaiting me.

"Way quah, what have you been doing?" These were the first words they spoke.

"Oh, I've just been looking after my traps," I told them.

"Your traps?" questioned my Uncle.

"Yes," I replied, "and I have a surprise for you. I set some traps all for myself. Look what I caught!" I held up my catch.

I was so excited I dropped my paddle. The current started carrying me away from the shore and on downstream. I didn't know what to do at the moment. So swift was the water it soon had the paddle out of my reach.

"Get down on the bottom of the boat," they called to me. "Use your hands for paddles."

This I did, and after much laughing from those who were watching me, I was able to recover my paddle. Soon I was safely on shore. Through it all they knew well enough that I was not in any real danger as long as they were near enough to come to my aid.

My heart was bursting with pride over what I had caught. It sang with the great joy I felt and the praise I knew that I now had the right to expect from these hunters. For surely they had not done any better on this day. I had trapped an animal that had beautiful fur, but as yet I had not the least idea what to name it. Besides this, I had also caught three muskrats and a small mink.

When finally I stepped on shore they came up, and it was easy to see they were really excited now. When I asked them what it was—this animal with the beautiful glossy fur—they said it was an otter.

For this they praised me and said that the pelt was worth fully $25.00.

Muskrats were only forty cents each, mink about $2.50, and coon not over a dollar. I had brought in more from one catch than all of them combined.

They skinned the otter for me, explaining that I didn't as yet know enough about such things and that we must not spoil the valuable pelt.

We remained at our camp for a week, for the trapping was good. We also needed this long rest from the tiresome canoe trip all the way from my uncle's.

On the night before we took our leave of this place where the trapping was so good, it was decided it was time to tell a story. I had done everything else so well that surely I would not disappoint them in my storytelling!

I got to thinking of the experience that Min di and Mother had with the big timber wolf the time of the snow storm, and I related this. The interest they showed encouraged me—so some of my bashfulness left me and I thought of a wolf story that I had learned from my books at the white man's school. I said I would tell them a real wolf story. Immediately their ears were open to what I would say.

"There was a little girl called Red Riding Hood," I began, "and I guess they called her that because she wore a red coat and red hood to keep her warm when the winter came. This little girl's home was on the edge of a great forest. One day her mother sent her with some cookies and things through this forest to the home of her grandmother. When the little girl got into the deep shadows made by the trees, she began to feel afraid. But, she thought, surely nothing could harm her if her mother had said she could go.

"But as she went on and on the shadows became deeper and deeper. She could not keep from feeling fear with every step. Before long she met a big wolf and he stopped her and asked, 'Where are you going, my little girl?'

" 'Oh, I'm going to see my grandmother. I must hurry.'

"The wolf let her go on, but he took another trail through the forest. He arrived at the grandmother's house before Red Riding Hood got there. The wolf ate the grandmother up and when the little girl finally came, he was in bed. On his head was grandmother's nightcap. He would make this little girl he had met in the forest think he was her grandmother.

"But she got out of the house before he could grab her and never stopped running until she ran in through the door of her own home. She told the terrible story of how a big bad wolf had eaten her dear grandmother."

That was the story as I remembered it. I knew that I had left out a lot, but my listeners thought it was good. They loved to hear stories of animals, and especially wolves.

CHAPTER XIII

IN THE morning following my telling of the story, we broke camp and paddled across the lake and on down the river again.

We had not gone far when we ran into a river drive. Logs were being floated down to the mills. All along the banks men were working to keep the logs moving. They went very slowly and there was constant work to be done to keep them from jamming in places.

I learned then that the two Indians who had come with us were very good river drivers. But in order to ride the logs they needed their spiked boots. Mack quah asked me if I would try and ride the logs for them, for I was light enough to do so with safety. Someone, they said, would have to clear these logs that were blocking our way.

Well, I had brought along some tennis shoes that they had given me in school. These I put on and it wasn't hard for me then to run the logs. When they were close together I had to push them apart and thus the canoe could go on through. It was a game for me. I liked it very much and was happy that it helped us to make headway.

I ran here and there over the great logs, jumping from one to another. Suddenly I missed my footing and went feet first into the water. I sank out of sight, but in a moment came up and there I was at the end of a log. They pulled me out a very chastened boy.

There were fully six miles of this. We did not

clear the last log until near the end of the second day. Trapping, of course, was out of the question during this time, and we just pushed on.

Finally we were in the farming country along the Mississippi, where there were many beautiful sights with the grain and corn growing in abundance. All we did during the next three days was eat, sleep, and paddle on and on. At last we came to Brainerd.

Each of us had fully $80 worth of furs, and here we sold the pelts, including that of the otter which I had trapped. First we took our bedding and equipment over to the railroad depot, for we decided to return on the train. The canoes we just turned over on dry land, where we left them. There would be plenty of time to make more canoes when later we needed them again. Always there would be an abundance of birch bark.

We were on our way back home, John Cloud and Mack quah going back to their families and Uncle Snow Cloud and I back to Mother.

Shortly after arriving home, my Uncle, seeing that Mother needed him, decided to live with her in the log cabin. He was a good provider, knowing so well the ways of the wild forest animals and how to grow the crops that must be added to the food supply.

Thus it was that we continued much in each other's company. Under his guidance I was getting experience that I might not otherwise have acquired. Gradually I was departing from the ways of the white man and reverting again more and more to the habits and customs of my people.

And thus the time passed and I reached the age of eighteen. It was then that one day Uncle told me of a moccasin game that was being played not far from our home.

"Would you like to go?" he asked me.

Naturally I did want to go. He promised that he would teach me the game. I had no money with which to play, for I had given all I had saved from the sale of my furs to Mother. But I could learn the game and see what I would win.

Early in the day we started out over a forest trail that led toward the setting sun. My spirits were high, for again I was going with my uncle to learn more of his teachings. Long before noon we neared this place of the game.

As we approached the clearing I could see a group squatting down outdoors, very much intent upon what they were doing.

"The game has already started," my uncle informed me. "You will see that they are playing outside now. But should it be stormy or cold they would go inside one of the large wigwams."

I soon learned that in this game, which was so popular with the Indians, there are usually five play-ers on each side. There may be even more con-testants, just so long as the sides remain even. Spread on the ground was a blanket, and on this the players squatted or sat. There were two drums and twenty sticks, the latter being half an inch in thickness and twelve to fifteen inches long. Each side had three sticks four or five feet in length and these were called "whips." Made from dry oak branches, they were whittled until very smooth and tapering.

Four buckskin moccasins were used to hide bullets under, and these bullets were something like marbles—three being exactly alike and the fourth slightly different in color or shape. It was this odd one that kept them guessing as to its exact location under the moccasins. The "moccasins" were only like a pattern of a moccasin from which the game gets its name. They were made of two thicknesses of buckskin sewed together. These were put in front of a player who sat in the middle of the others. He was called the "hider."

While yet we were coming up to the settlement, I had wondered at the sound of drums but had said nothing at the time. Now, however, I noticed that in the midst of the group we now watched were two drums, one on either side of the Indian who was the "hider." While this man shifted the bullets around under the moccasins, two men kept up a monotonous beating of drums. So as I watched, this middle man hid the bullets to the accompaniment of the drums. During this there was constant chanting by this manager of the drum sticks.

The whips, I learned, were used to strike or lift up the moccasin under which they thought the odd bullet was hidden. If they lifted and tossed back a moccasin, that meant the bullet was not there. But should they strike at the moccasin, that indicated it was there. When they lifted the moccasin and the marked bullet was there, they paid eight sticks from their pile of twenty. Again they would hide the bullets and then take their whips to lift a moccasin. If the bullet was not there they raised another moccasin. If still the bullet was not there, they had one more chance. This they used to whip down on one of the remaining moccasins. If again they missed, it cost them six sticks. Now they hid again and if they raised one moccasin and hit down on one of the three that remained and still missed, they paid four sticks.

Again they hid the bullet. As their sticks were getting low, one of the players held up two fingers and took the whip and struck down on the moccasin. If the bullet were there, then the other side would take over the moccasins and drums. It would be their turn to do the hiding.

Thus they play back and forth until one side loses all its sticks, twenty, and that is called a game. These twenty sticks are then exchanged by the winning side for a smaller, but carved or notched, stick.

Sometimes this game goes on day and night for three or four days, or just as long as the contestants want to continue. The opposite players watching the "hiding man" will see him move a finger maybe. Or it might be the merest twitching of a muscle, or swaying of his body, or any movement that suggests his letting loose the bullet from his hand. Some of the prizes for which they played may be listed as follows:

For eight games—medicine bag; pony; headdress; dancing costume.

For six games—buckskin shirt.

For four games—blankets.

For two games—pair of moccasins; pair of gloves.

For one game—ten pounds of rice; five pounds maple sugar.

As I continued to watch, my Uncle explained the different parts of the game that I could not so easily understand. It looked so easy to guess where the players had put the bullet.

But shortly my chance came to enter the game, and I was soon to learn that it was not nearly as easy as it appeared. The man had a way of slipping the elusive bullet under the moccasin where one was least likely to look.

At the end of this first day of the game I became very friendly with an Indian named Fairweather. He was large of bone, tall, and very thin. He had wavy hair, and his eyes were as blue as the noonday sky. All that day he had not worn his coat, but carried it on his arm.

We went off together toward one of the stores and as we walked along, he asked me:

"Do you happen to have any relatives up around Cass Lake?"

"Why do you ask?" I wanted to know.

"Well, there is a man there who looks just like you—only he is older."

"My father lives at Cass Lake," I told him. "Can you tell me about him? I have seen him only once since I started to the white man's school."

"About all I know is that this man had nearly a

hundred men working for him every winter in the logging camp. He is well known and well liked."

"Was his name Pin de gay gisgig?" I asked.

"Yes, that was his name."

"My name is Way quah gisgig," I told him. "He and my Mother have not lived together for many years."

"Why don't you go up there?" he suggested. "You could make money working for him and send some home to your mother."

"How could I get there?" I inquired. I was interested.

"I'll write your father," he promised. "Maybe he will send you the train fare."

Two weeks passed. Then came a letter in the mail. It was from my father, and enclosed in the envelope was money for my fare to take me to him. That night, as we sat together in the big room of the cabin, I could not bear to tell Mother that I was leaving the home she had made for me. I would be the last of her children to go, and she would have no one left but Uncle. I knew then that I was going to Father, but he had said when we had met him at the school that no word about him should go to our Mother. That was what he had told Bishiu.

So the next day I took the money Father had sent and with it I bought groceries.

"But where did you get the money?" Mother wanted to know when I gave her the food.

So pleased was she that I could not tell her the truth.

"I earned it." I lied to her. I wanted so much to make her happy, but I knew that I must go to where Father was waiting for me. Perhaps I was selfish— but I had grown up by now. Much of my life had been spent away from home already, and surely she would not miss me so much; not with Uncle Snow Cloud there to see that she wanted for nothing.

The leaves of the trees had already turned brown and fallen to the bare, cold ground. The first snow had come to forest and field, and the long winter was upon us. The north wind blew its frosty breath over the many lakes, and even now there was a thin coating of ice.

Ever since getting the letter from Father, I had been restless and had wanted to go to him, but always I would think of Mother. I was supposed to be the head of the family, and I could not so easily leave. One day, however, the urge was strong upon me. Even the wind seemed to sing through the pine needles for me to go. Father had called me and I should go. Mother would be safe and well provided for by my Uncle. This was the argument that per-suaded me that now was the time.

Not far away was the railroad, and I imagined I heard its whistle calling "Come . . . come." Already I had been given my train fare and had turned it over to Mother. There was the problem of how to get to Father? I had heard of white boys going on freight trains. Why not I?

Getting together some food and bundle of clothes, I started out over the forest trail in the direction of the railroad. That afternoon I was perched on top of a freight car bound for Cass Lake and the home of my father. The car tops were slippery from snow and frozen rain, and the wind at times threatened to sweep me off. Soon I was almost frozen, and so I sought the cover of a boxcar where in comparative comfort I finished the trip.

When at last I got off at Cass Lake I was stiff from the cold, but happy that now I would see my father. In front of a feed store was an old Indian. He was loading some food in his sleigh. My first thought was that he was a medicine man, and I was afraid. Ever since my sickness at school, I had not wanted them around me—even though at the time it was a medicine man who had saved my life.

The old man stopped for a moment in his loading and said, "You look like Pin de gay gishig. Are you the son that he has been expecting?"

"It is true," I replied. "I am Way quah gishig, his oldest son. Where can I find my father?"

"It is only a little while since your father left here. He was loading up some food and when he had finished he drove off. Wait until I finish and I'll drive you over to the other store where you may find him."

I got into his sleigh and went with him. At the hitching rail of the store where he took me was a pair of buckskin horses.

"That's your father's team," the Indian said, pointing. "He may be in the store. I'll go see."

I followed him inside and there stood my father at the counter. The old man called, "I found your son down at the other store. Now I'll go."

Father came over to me and said, "You've grown into a man since last I saw you at the school. It is well that you have come to me."

And I am glad to come to the home of my father," I replied.

After a moment he looked down at my feet. "Are not your feet cold?" he inquired. "What is that you are wearing?"

"They are overshoes. I had no other shoes of the white man's making, and I had not prepared warm moccasins for the winter."

"Come with me," he instructed, and we went to the clothing department where he told the store keeper to get me a complete outfit, from cap to shoes, and extra warm underwear. When finally I was dressed up in these new clothes, my father said:

"Have you had anything to eat since you left home?"

"Oh, yes," I assured him. "But now you have taken all the food I brought, for it was in my old clothes." It was the rice, jerky meat and maple sugar with which I had filled my pockets before leaving home.

"Then you must come with me. The horses are well covered and we will go to the restaurant where I always eat."

The warm meal was welcome after my long, cold ride on the freight train, and as I sat there in the warm building away from the chill wind I felt very grateful to this father of mine whom until now I had known so little. There he sat at the counter in his great fur coat. It was long and heavy with a high collar that he could pull up around his face and over his ears. He said it was made of calfskin. Father was tall and strong and raw-boned, like one accustomed to hard work.

As I looked at him, I thought, "Osh kin has nothing on me now. My father has this beautiful team of horses and he hires many men to help him with his work. He must really be a great man among these people!" I was proud to be seen with him and to have him call me Neeo gob bo, which meant "outstanding." This was the name Father always used for me.

When finally the meal was over, we went into the cold and snow. Outside, the beautiful buckskin horses were hitched in front of Taylor's Department Store. I sat in front with Father on the feed sacks. He handed me the reins:

"Wouldn't you like to drive?" he asked.

Proudly I took the lines. What a beautiful, spirited pair of horses they were! They proved to be so lively I had to hold on tight or they would have run away.

We drove in the ever-deepening snow for about an hour. The road led through the forest where all the trees and bushes were covered with snow. The great north wind had come with its icy breath and left a beautiful blanket of whiteness that only the smile of the warm sun could take away.

We came to a lake—a smooth, barren place covered with new snow. Here Father got out and said, "I'll go ahead and make sure that the ice will hold up our team and load."

He took his axe to test the ice and added, "Don't start until I get a little distance ahead of you. Then just follow my tracks."

There were about three inches of snow on the ice, and every other step he would hit down with his axe through the snow, so as to get the sound of the ice for its thickness. By this method he learned whether or not the lake was safe for our crossing. If there was an air pocket, as often was the case, he would make a detour. And always, as he directed, I remained a safe distance behind him.

Soon we crossed over the lake and were back on the trail. This road we followed through the forest until finally we came to another lake.

"This is Loss Lake," he told me. "See those buildings over there? That is our home."

The house was a two-story log building, and it was not more than half a mile from the lake shore.

When shortly we drove up to the front door, we could see some of the family looking out at us through the frosty windows. Just as we started for the door they came out to meet us.

"This is Awani ga," said my Father, indicating a boy who was short and with heavy brown eyes. "And this is She wan," taking in a short, pug-nosed little girl by the hand. She had very black, straight hair and her eyes held a mischievous look.

We went on into the house, where he introduced me to my stepmother.

"Nee o gob bo has come to live with us," he told her. "Where are the other children?"

"They have gone to a neighbor's house to play in the snow," she said. "They will be here soon."

There were three children besides the two I had met: Gegwe tah, a brother; Dahnainee, the middle sister; and Mazini, the oldest girl. That made two boys and three girls.

My stepmother was very pleasant and talked freely to me. I knew at once she was glad to have me with them, even though she did have a large family. But for awhile I was very bashful in my new surroundings.

My new mother was short and rather stout. Her hair was parted in the middle and there was one long braid hanging down her back. Her eyes were brown and her face was very pretty. I liked her instantly. Maybe it was because she made me feel that I was really wanted.

"You are going to be a big help to me," she said. "You can get in the wood and maybe help some with the smaller children. Then there are the cows to milk and the pigs to feed. We are busy all the time and there is much to be done. At times your father will need you to drive to the logging camp so you can bring the team home for use here if it is needed."

I heard some music coming from a room just off the kitchen where we sat around the stove trying to keep warm. I learned that it was from a cylinder gramophone.

When the recording was finished. Mother went

in and put on another one. The song that now floated out to me was called "Back to Mother's Knee." As I listened I thought of my own Mother back there in the log cabin. She was no doubt wondering by now where I had gone and was waiting for me to come home! Poor Mother! Already she had lost three children by death—and now the three who were left had gone from her fireside. She had only Uncle Snow Cloud, and perhaps he would not remain with her always.

Later in the day the other children came home from their play at the neighbor's. Instantly I knew that I liked Mazini very much. She was the oldest of the sisters. Although I was much the older, we would have many things in common. Perhaps she would even help me to forget my loss of Bishiu.

From the very beginning, Father and I had many talks on matters that had to do with the deeper things of life.

"What church do you go to?" he inquired a few days after my arrival.

"Well," I told him. "I have been going to the Episcopal Church. It is only because I was told to go there, though. I have never been able to accept many of the teachings of this church or of any other church of the white man."

"Then you have never forgotten the teachings of our people, my son, and it is well."

"What you say is true, Father. I still believe in and worship the Great Spirit, and His messages have come to me often while I sat under the spreading oak or walked the forest trails where the tall pines bent their heads to the strong wind. There I listened to the messages that the Great Spirit might send. I have watched the wild rose push its head up through the deep moss in the shadows that the forest makes. I have seen the flowers peep up through the leaves and twigs of the forest floor. It is in these that I have felt the presence of the One who alone can help me in my troubles."

My father nodded understandingly. "So long as you really understand these things and listen well to His voice, there is no need of what the white man calls a church in which to worship. For our people believe that we enter church when we are born. It is in our body, and in order to keep this church clean and pure, we should be very careful what we put in our mouth, or how we take care of the body that was given us."

On this day we talked a long time on this subject, and it became clearer to me now than ever before why I had never been able to believe what the white man tried to teach me as a substitute for the beliefs of my own people.

"Now that you are to live with me," Father said, "you can worship the Great Spirit with the rest of us. This evening I shall get my drum and we will sound for the Great Spirit to be with us."

This drum of which Father spoke was a special kind of drum. Great care is taken to pick out a basswood log. Sometimes one is found that is hollow, but if that is impossible, one is hollowed out. The tree used for this purpose is about twelve inches in diameter and from this a block eighteen inches long is cut. When this block is hollowed, it is put in water to soak thoroughly. Maybe this soaking will take a month, so it is placed in the river or lake where it is watched closely. After a time, the bark falls off or slides off, and this portion is put where it will dry slowly. Sometimes if the weather is too hot, it is buried, and this process requires about two weeks. The block is then scraped smooth, both inside and out, and a flat piece of oak is wedged into one end to make the bottom. Buckskin is wrapped around both bottom and top to keep it firm. And again the drum thus fashioned is watched by the owner so that it will never be allowed to dry out and perhaps fall to pieces. There is a crossbar near the top, and when not in use, the top buckskin is laid on these crossbars. When the time comes to use the drum, water is put in the bottom and the skin is then stretched over the top.

CHAPTER XIV

IN THE EVENING we had a wonderful meal. The chores were finished and the family all gathered around the fireplace in the living room.

Father now fixed his drum and brought out a long piece of birch bark that had been stripped down to a heavy paper. His wife was on one side of him and I was on the other. The five children sat behind us, as it is not the custom to sit in a circle.

Now he put this strip of bark, about which I was very curious, in front of him and held it down with rocks to keep it flat.

"This is a chart," he explained to me, "that has been handed down to me through many generations of our peoples. It is said to be fully six hundred years old. Since you are the oldest of my children, it is my wish that this chart shall go to you, as will also the drum. Of the chart I shall teach you all I know. Study it closely."

Bending over this ancient chart of birch bark I noticed that it was covered with many strange drawings. Dotting the skyline were symbols of the sun, the moon, and the stars. There was also a symbol of the cross, and this seemed to resemble a man with his arm outstretched. These arms denoted the act of embracing, to accept anything that the Great Spirit had put on earth. The upright piece, which pointed to heaven, urged that people live righteously during this life on earth. There were rocks and this meant a strong foundation.

After the cross came symbols of men, men of different tribes. Many other strange symbols there were, some that I cannot remember. But I do recall a long knife, or sword. This, Father explained, was the symbol of the white man's coming and of how these paleface brothers would cut and destroy the friendship that might otherwise have always existed between the Indian tribes and those who had come to live in their lands. I could easily understand this, for the Chippewas have a custom of never giving or receiving any sharp or cutting weapon or instrument, for this would be a sign of the parting of friends.

The chart showed how step by step the white men would gradually take from us our land and finally destroy all the beauty and harmony that generations of our people had handed down to us. They would kill the wildlife and cut down our forests. They would plow the land and clear the trees and brush and in many other ways change things so that the Indian could no longer live as he had been taught by his ancestors. This was why the white man was called Kitchee-mokoman, or the great knife or sword.

Down lower on the page a few lines was a figure that would be a steamboat. "Here," Father explained, "is the symbol that the Indians could not know about until a steamboat appeared on one of the lakes and rivers.

Still farther down on the chart was the symbol that meant war, a war between the white man and the Indians, for Bear Island, about the year 1893.

There were markings that indicated men flying in the air, far above the clouds. At that time we had not even heard of airplanes. This was about one-third of the way down the chart. Many more symbols followed, which must have meant that even to this day the things this chart included in its many strange symbols have not come to pass.

To me all this was very interesting as we sat there before the flickering, crackling fire with Father explaining as best he could about this chart of birch bark that had come into his hands. That night the spirit of our ancestors seemed to hover very close.

I asked more about how he had come to possess this chart and felt it was an honor indeed for him to offer it to me that I should keep it during my time on earth. He had been offered a huge sum for it, but had refused to part with it. No amount of money, he said, could buy it. (But the time came later when Father did part with this birch-bark chart. And that day was the saddest of his life. The chart was stolen and until this day it had not been recovered. I still live in hopes that the Great Spirit will guide the one who now has this sacred document to my door, so that I may go on with the great work for my people where my Father left off.)

In the days that followed, Father taught me many things that added to my understanding. I, too, learned how to sound for the Great Spirit, as we had about eight chants between moons. He explained that during these sessions he would be told just what the various symbols on the chart meant. More than once he would want to find out something special and would call the family together. On these occasions, as at the weekly sessions, he would beat the drum, and this would be done to drown out all other sounds, or as if a curtain were being drawn about us. Only in this way could the sounds or vibrations that we were waiting for come through to our consciousness. And always during these times was the chart spread out before him, or rolled up if there was no reason at the moment to study it further. When not in use, the chart was rolled up and tied with wegoob, or buckskin, and placed on top of all supplies for that particular week.

In front of the drum was placed a skin or hide of some animal that had recently been killed. Any other hides or furs from animals that had been caught were piled on this skin. Or, if there had been a rice-gathering or berry-picking, these too were added. Never was any kind of machine-made article deposited here. This was a symbol of thankfulness, or a prayer of gratitude to the Great Spirit for giving one the power to receive these messages. Father told us that we, too, would get these messages if we listened well to what the Great Spirit was trying to tell us. He called it a vibration to which we must atune our hearts, and all who had faith and waited with the expectation of receiving only good would know exactly what to do. Religion always came from within and all children of the Great Spirit had equal power to receive His blessings.

Winter passed quickly. The heavy snows that had blanketed forest and lake melted under the breath of the warm winds and the bright sun. Streams and rivers were full to overflowing. New, green grass began to appear around the edges of lakes and in open fields where the sun was brightest. O pee chee, the robin, lent his happy voice to the songs of the spring. Other birds followed and sang their chorus of gladness for the new life that was budding everywhere.

We moved from Loss Lake to Rice Lake, and when the sap first started to flow, we went to the sugar bush. I had learned well my lessons in sugar making from Mother, but now I found that the work was much more interesting here with Father. For now we had horses and thus could go farther and get more of the sap, since we did not have to carry it in the birch-bark containers. Now, too, we could reach more trees, and that required more kettles for boiling.

Came the warm days of mid-summer which brought with them the ripening berries. We took the horses and went far into the woods. The crop this year was abundant, and we carried home from our various trips enough of the fruit so that many bushels were sold to the stores in town.

When the rice-gathering started in early fall, we went into the lake with several canoes and returned with great loads of this food that was so important to the Indian during the winter months when the snow was deepest and the earth lay cold and dead. We lived right on the shore of the lake, so it was not necessary to camp out during the harvesting. There were others though who came to camp on our land, for Father let it be known they were welcome. During the rice season there was always quite a crowd of people around.

Then came the time when the rice-gathering was over. Many of the leaves had already shed their bright coloring and they lay thick on the forest floor.

Shortly now another winter would be upon us,

and it was almost a year since I had come to live with my father. Most of the hard work of storing away food for the cold months was over, and some of the older folks decided upon having a medicine dance.

On this important occasion, as always, Father was to be the leader (Grand Medicine Man). If there arose any trouble in the gathering, those involved would come to him to straighten it out. Also, he was the one to decide when and where to hold the dance. To my questions he said, "We will have it in about ten days now. It will be near the shores of Cass Lake, on a little bluff there overlooking the water."

This information he gave to all those who wanted to go, and they returned to their homes. Before we left, however, Father hired several Indians to cut hay on Turtle River, a little way above Rice Lake. This work was to be done with scythes, and he left a man in charge, one he had trusted with the job the fall before.

It was time now for us to start for the appointed place—the bluff on Cass Lake—and as we drove along my heart sang with joy. For me it was to be perhaps the greatest occasion of my entire life. A family that had arrived before us had already found a location they thought would be right.

"Come over here," they called as we approached the bluff. "Do you not think this spot would be right for your wigwam?"

Father and Mother climbed down from the wagon, and we six children scampered out after

147

them. Just below were the sparkling waters of the
lake, and all around were towering pines and several spreading oaks whose branches by now were
almost bare of the leaves that had fallen and made a
beautiful soft carpet underneath. On this day, the
wind blew gently through the pine needles and
seemed to whisper a message of peace and good will.
Chipmunks watched with alert, cunning eyes as
they hunted acorns and other nuts for storage in
their own little homes high up in the protecting
trees.

Dad answered the question about our wigwam
by saying, "Yes, this is about the place. As for the
medicine wigwam, it can be built just beyond where
there are no trees or stumps."

Looking around I saw that many other Indian
families had already gathered for the big occasion.
Even now most of them were busy building their
wigwams or putting up tents. They had come from
up and down the river, mostly by wagon.

Before the sun had gone down behind the thick
forest growth, the Medicine Dance Village was
started. It was the custom and a long-established religious fact that no one could help in this building
except those who were devout believers. So Father
had picked those he knew were suited for this purpose. The wigwam near the center of this village
was the place where Father would sit during the
ceremonies. No one but the two other medicine
men and he could enter this sacred place.

Next morning, as the work went on, poles were
put all around and bent over like bows, thus form-

ing a half-loop about five feet high. These were put in the ground at a regular distance apart, so close that no one could walk through, but all could see beyond into the grounds. Each loop was made to cross at a certain angle.

The entrance hall was soon finished, and in all this building I was trying to do my share. Indeed, the knowledge gained while I lived with Mother and went about with my uncle was valuable to me now, and I did not find it hard to hold my own with the best of them.

I noticed symbols of animals or crosses on the posts. Father was there in his wigwam that was built to one side. There he had taken his drum, the chart, and a few other things he would need. The first day he spent in drumming and singing his chants. He stayed there till darkness came to the nearby forest and spread over bluff and lake.

The second day of the ceremonies was the receiving day. Leading the procession was Wind i go wab with his wife and two daughters. If one wanted to join, he must be in line this day. Each must have a skin or hide of some animal, fish, or fowl that had been stuffed with rice or dried food. It is a symbol of gratitude for the food. As the people were accepted by the medicine man, who was appointed by Father, they lined up by the entrance, which was on the east side of the wigwam, and they were asked questions about their belief. Then they were left standing inside the hall. When finally all had been received, then the medicine man stepped in with them. He passed on by to the other medicine man who said if there was any one who wanted to stop, now was the time to do so, as they passed the west gate.

For this procession there was a certain step, which, I learned, was the medicine dance step. It was something like a hesitation step and was meant to tell the Great Spirit that they were coming. If they just stepped along quietly the Great Spirit would not "feel" them, but in this way they sent out a sort of vibration. Now they stepped along until they came to the symbol of an animal. Here they stopped to put a few grains of rice or food from their containers on a shelf built especially for this purpose. Then again they moved around the hall and a third time around the Grand Medicine Man, and another medicine man met them in front of the wigwam, where they took their containers or stuffed animals. Here the medicine man laid the offerings on the ground near the Grand Medicine man's (my father's) wigwam. He sent them to the cross with this thought:

"Can you face the cross, believing it is a human being, with your arms outstretched to embrace the world and go straight? If so, go forward."

There by the cross they lingered either in prayer or just in thankfulness. Then they walked around again in exactly the same manner, with that peculiar step. The Grand Medicine Man then went back into the wigwam, and all the containers were brought in.

Father sat and beat his drum and chanted his songs as the medicine man brought the containers out to whomever they belonged, and these came forward to receive them. Then they stepped down the hall towards the entrances, where they passed out one by one, still in the same dance step. Now they were members in good standing.

The third day was the time for the parents to bring their children. This did not mean that the children belonged; they must decide for themselves later, when they were old enough. But now it was more to have the Great Spirit see and bless them.

The fourth day was the medicine day. Father held a birch-bark container or basket, into which each one puts his medicine or herbs. They had to remember what they had put in so they would get their own things back after Father had taken them into the wigwam where he sang and beat the drum. This was not a worship of any god or image, but was simply a petition to the Great Spirit that he should make it known whether this was a good medicine for a particular ailment. They would go to the cross then, where, in meditation or prayer, they would get the vibration that would inform them whether this particular medicine was what they needed for a cure.

Meanwhile, the folks would stand out in the hall in prayerful attitude. They visited with one another and all seemed to have a good time. Each told the other what they thought his own special medicine would accomplish in the way of cures. Each was willing to share these medicines with any who wished them.

After this fourth day of the ceremonies was over the people just sat around talking and eating. One or two of the new members arranged to put on a feast. This had been planned ahead of the gathering. Someone on the outside had it all prepared, and now they brought it to the receiving line. These two members went to meet them and brought the food into the hall, then proceeded to serve the others waiting for the feast. Each had his own container made of birchbark.

While those who were in the hall enjoyed the feast, the others on the ground had prepared their fires and had their feast, too. There were people from distant places, even white folks coming to look on and learn of the ways of the Indian.

I sat by the side of my Father on the seat of the wagon as we made our way home after the festivities.

The sun commenced to sink behind the forest as we headed home. The children were asleep in the back of the wagon and Father was strangely silent. Somehow the whole world seemed to be holding still for a moment to listen to the voice of the Great Spirit.

Never before had I felt so near to my beloved Bishiu and the others who had passed on. Then suddenly it seemed that Bishiu came to the edge of the forest and was standing looking over at me with a smile on her lips.

Her voice came to me as clear as crystal. "Way quah," she said, "You are ready for manhood . . . many events await you. Love will come into your life . . . already a girl awaits . . . but always remember, I shall be ever at your side, as we promised!"

I passed my hand across my brow. When I looked over again the vision was gone.

The paper on which this book is printed bears the watermark of the University of Oklahoma Press and has an effective life of at least three hundred years.